WHEN TIME
IS SHORT

◆

WHEN TIME IS SHORT

IS SHORT

◆

FINDING OUR WAY
IN THE ANTHROPOCENE

◆

TIMOTHY BEAL

Beacon Press
BOSTON

BEACON PRESS
Boston, Massachusetts
www.beacon.org

Beacon Press books
are published under the auspices of
the Unitarian Universalist Association of Congregations.

25 24 23 22   8 7 6 5 4 3 2 1

This book is printed on acid-free paper that meets the uncoated paper
ANSI/NISO specifications for permanence as revised in 1992.

Text design and composition by Kim Arney

Library of Congress Cataloging-in-Publication Data is available for this title.
Library of Congress Control Number: 2022001446
Hardcover ISBN: 978-0-8070-9000-8
Ebook ISBN: 978-0-8070-9001-5

For my students
in Religion and Ecology

CONTENTS

INTRODUCTION
WITH PLAYLIST

T HIS IS A BOOK about our denial of death as a species. It's also about how religion, especially Christianity, has fueled that denial, and how religion might offer resources to help break through it, to live into our finite human future in a more humble, mindful, and meaningful way.

When I tell friends that I'm writing a book about "our denial of death as a species," they sometimes think that what I mean is "our denial, as a species, of death." That I'm writing about how we humans tend to live in denial of our own mortality. There is a wonderful book on that subject: Ernest Becker's *The Denial of Death*, which won the 1974 Pulitzer Prize for General Non-Fiction two months after Becker himself died of colon cancer. That book's influence on this one is great. I have spent a lot of time with it over the past several years.

But that's not what this book is about. When I say, "our denial of death as a species," I'm not talking about our denial, as a species, of mortality, but rather our denial of the mortality of our species. Our denial of the very real and imminent potential for human extinction. I want to explore on the species level what Becker was exploring on the individual level.

This is not another "before it's too late" book. This is a "what if it's already too late?" book. Maybe it's not. But what if it is? What if we, along with many other plants and animals, have fifty years, or two hundred years, or maybe even several hundred more years left?

What if we consider, even for a moment, that our faith in ourselves to engineer or science our way out of this is unreliable, perhaps even delusional? What then? How should we live?

FAITH IN THE ANTHROPOCENE

Only lately have we started to acknowledge the very real possibility, I daresay probability, that humankind will literally wear out its welcome on the planet. There have been five great extinction events on Earth. This would be the sixth, and the only one brought about by those being extinguished. On this horizon, new and emerging voices in science, philosophy, religion, and art are inviting us, sometimes pushing us, to imagine a post-human world.[1] We are being called to recognize our place in history in terms of the era of the Anthropocene.

The term "Anthropocene" was coined in the year 2000 to underscore the fact that we are now living in a world in which anthropogenic (human-originating) forces have as much or more impact on the planet's ecological and geological systems as nonhuman forces do. Scholars debate exactly when the Anthropocene officially succeeded the Holocene as Earth's new geological era. Some say it was at the dawn of capitalism and European colonial expansion during the seventeenth century. Others say it started with the industrial revolution and the invention of the steam engine in the eighteenth century. Most, including a team of scientists called the Anthropocene Working Group, say it began right around 1945, with the first atomic bombs and the "Great Acceleration," which was marked by unprecedented alterations to Earth's biological and hydrological systems brought about by exponential population growth and the global rise of large-scale industrial societies.[2] A quick Internet image search for the phrase "Great Acceleration" will pull up a host of graphs that powerfully illustrate this rapid escalation beginning in the middle of the twentieth century, from urban populations to gross domestic products, from great floods per decade to deforestation, from international travel activity to the number of McDonald's restaurants.

Millions of years from now, the geological evidence marking this new era will be the "stratigraphic signatures" we leave behind: huge deposits of concrete, plastic, carbon, and nuclear fallout.[3] Such will be our geological legacy, our signature layer, on the planet. "Humans were here."

Whenever the Anthropocene officially began, we are now in it, and there is no going back. Not only does this fact push us to recognize that we humans are now the primary cause of geological and ecological change, including climate change. It also has the potential to remind us that there was something *before* us and there will be something *after* us. In fact, although we are responsible for the Anthropocene, it will outlast us; we will continue to affect the planet long after the last humans are gone. Recognizing that we are now living in the Anthropocene, then, invites us also to reflect on a post-human, eventually post-Anthropocene, future for the planet.

And why is that so hard to conceive, so easy to deny? More than 99 percent of all species that have ever lived on the planet are now extinct. Why, then, is it nearly impossible to imagine a world without us—a thriving post-human creation?

I have to admit that I have a hard time talking about all this with friends and colleagues, let alone strangers. When I was working on this book, I asked my students in a college course I teach on religion and ecology to read a rough draft of it. I was surprised by how self-conscious I felt as I struggled to introduce it to them. I was even more uneasy as I waited for their responses. In the end, I'm very glad I did share it. Their insightful and critical engagement with it, and with me, has been both encouraging and challenging.

I still feel a little uneasy and self-conscious to be putting this book out there. Why? Is it because I worry that it could be a buzzkill? Or that it actually sounds crazy? Or is it because my conflict-avoidant personality is once again in conflict with my desire to pursue uncomfortable questions? Yes, yes, and yes. But I suspect that something else is also going on. I suspect that I have so deeply internalized the denial I'm writing about that part of me wants to censor my own voice. I want to police my own thoughts as not only unbelievable but unthinkable. Denial is strong enough in and around me that I am fighting against my own will to break through it.

REREADING RELIGION

A big part of the drive to deny, I believe, is religious.

Becker and others have shown how religion often feeds our denial of death as individuals by providing the tools and materials to build "immortality vehicles," or "immortality projects," for transcending our dreadful fate as food for worms. From repaying worldly suffering with heavenly reward, to furthering the divine will through sacrifice in holy war, to infinitely extending our biological shelf life through technology, all our immortality vehicles are religious.

I believe that religion also has a great deal to do with our denial of human finitude and death as a species. By religion, I mean a specific, highly distilled form of modern Western Christian theology, one that is rooted in a tiny handful of Bible verses. It is the theology of human exceptionalism. This is the idea or rather the belief in our godlike dominion over the natural world as humans, that humankind is exceptional to the rest of creation. This is our theological origin story, the founding myth of the modern West. It is also the unacknowledged, little understood, yet fundamental sustaining faith that drives global capitalism, whose Anthropocenic dream of infinite growth through extraction is driving and drilling us to an early extinction.

As I will argue, this religion of godlike human exceptionalism is a modern invention. However biblical or Christian it claims to be, this worldview would have been alien and unbelievable to the traditions and perspectives of those peoples it considers its ancestors. I want to recover those earlier traditions and perspectives in biblical tradition, as well as traces of even earlier indigenous religious cultures behind them. In so doing I hope to un-read them from the perspective of the dominion delusion they've been forced to serve, and to re-read them for what insights they might have to offer us today. Far

from promoting godlike human exceptionalism, many of these traditions, I find, are closer to what the Buddhist poet and environmental
philosopher-activist Gary Snyder calls "the practice of the wild" than
modern Christianity has been able to recognize.[4] This is largely because modern Christianity has taken such pains to try to distance
its inherited traditions from other "primitive" indigenous religions.
Rereading these traces of the biblical-aboriginal on the horizon of
human finitude, I find that they speak to the cultivation of what I call
earth creatureliness, a spiritual worldview characterized by interdependence and impermanence.

Some might nonetheless ask why we should bother to revisit biblical tradition in search of alternative religious and theological perspectives on our late-human world. Even if they have been misread
in the service of dominionism and human exceptionalism, so what?
Why not just move on? Fair questions.

When it comes to facing our denial of death as a species and a
limited human future on the planet, I think most of us are still in the
early stages of shock. Much like someone who has just lost a loved
one or been given a devastating diagnosis, we are stupefied, at a loss
for words. We cannot quite fathom the new reality, let alone what
life will be like from now on. We have no vocabulary to navigate our
way forward.

Part of the reason for revisiting these religious traditions, then, is
to begin to find language for our new reality. Not that I think these
traditions have everything we will need. We should be searching
everywhere, past and present, for handles and toeholds, for ways to
create new imaginative spaces from the remains of what we have inherited. Doing so with these biblical traditions speaks to that task,
even as it exposes how unstable they were as foundations for our faith
in human exceptionalism.

Implicit here is an argument about what religion is. Religion is
not simply about adhering to or following some fixed set of prescribed
doctrines and practices. Religion is above all an ongoing process of
meaning making. Religion is interpretation all the way down. As its

Latin roots in *religare* ("re-bind," "re-member," "re-connect") and *relegere* ("re-read") suggest, religion is reading and rereading, connecting and reconnecting, imaginatively re-membering our world. It is fundamentally about creatively reinterpreting and remaking inherited traditions—scriptures, ideas, beliefs, practices, and institutions—in light of new and emerging horizons of meaning.

So too with the Bible. The Bible is not a book, let alone The Book. Nor does it present anything like a single, unified story or voice. As I have argued elsewhere, the Bible is not a book of answers but a library of questions.[5] When we actually crack it open and try to read it, what we find is a rich collection of different, often conflicting voices and worldviews representing thousands of human hands and thousands of years of ancient oral and literary history. It is a polyvocal (many-voiced) tradition that not only is comfortable with contradictions and differences but canonizes them.

Part of the task, then, will be to reexamine, reread, and reinterpret the scriptural traditions that have been claimed as foundational to the modern faith in godlike dominion and human exceptionalism. After centuries of reciting them in service of this faith, they have become almost inseparable from it. We need to estrange ourselves from what we think we know about these texts and traditions in order to reread and remember them with fresh eyes, to bring them back down to earth. As Lynn White Jr. famously put it at the end of his now canonical 1967 essay, "The Historical Roots of Our Ecologic Crisis," if religion has gotten us into this mess, religion has to be part of the way out.

> Both our present science and our present technology are so tinctured with orthodox Christian arrogance toward nature that no solution for our ecologic crisis can be expected from them alone. Since the roots of our trouble are so largely religious, the remedy must also be essentially religious, whether we call it that or not. We must rethink and refeel our nature and destiny.[6]

White proposed that we make the medieval mystic monk Francis of Assisi, who talked to animals and called the moon his sister and the sun his brother, our ecological patron saint. He argued that Francis represented an early form of what we now call Christian panentheism, a theology that sees the world and God as interrelated, with God in the world and the world in God. As ecofeminist theologian Sallie McFague puts it, panentheistic theology insists on both "the most radical transcendence and the most radical immanence," bringing "God and the world together in the most intimate and total way—taking my 'matter' into God's own self," and vice versa.[7] Such an approach, Dorothy Dean has shown, opens up an ecotheological understanding of what it means to be human that is not only "anti-anthropocentric but truly non-exceptionalistic," in which humans are "part of the 'flesh' of the world." "We only exist," she writes, "as this relationship between our individual bodily flesh and the flesh of the world."[8]

A little over a decade after White's nomination of Francis as the patron saint of ecotheology, Pope John Paul II proclaimed him the "heavenly Patron of those who promote ecology." I am on board with that, as I am with McFague's and Dean's more fully developed ecotheology. But I also want to look deeper into the earlier traditions that shaped the likes of Francis. What might he have been seeing there that we may be missing? I believe it goes all the way back to surviving traces of an early indigenous religiosity, still discoverable in these ancient scriptures.

O CHILDREN

I like to do my research and writing alongside and in conversation with music. For me, this kind of dialogue opens up space that is generative for critical reflection, not only about the subject I'm exploring but also about why I care enough to spend so much time and energy trying to write about it.

While working on this book, I've had a playlist of songs on heavy rotation.[9] Many were first shared with me by students and friends at different stages of my work and have become so integrated with this project that I no longer know them apart from it. Many of you will understand that. Indeed, for many of you, seeing the playlist might be more revealing of what this book is about than any written introduction could ever be. So, for what it's worth, here it is, as of now:

"The Future," by Leonard Cohen
"Big Exit," by PJ Harvey
"O Children," by Nick Cave and the Bad Seeds
"My Name Is Dark," by Grimes
"Lampshades on Fire," by Modest Mouse
"After the Gold Rush," by Dolly Parton (covering Neil Young)
"Ideoteque," by Radiohead
"Darkseid," by Grimes and 潘PAN
"XXX," by Kendrick Lamar
"Last Great American Whale," by Lou Reed
"Dystopia (The Earth Is on Fire)," by YACHT
"The Earth Died Screaming," by Tom Waits
"The Apocalypse Song," by St. Vincent
"Long Way Down," by Robert DeLong
"God's Gonna Cut You Down," by Johnny Cash
"From God's Perspective," by Bo Burnham
"Hurt," by Nine Inch Nails
"Pink Moon," by Nick Drake
"State of the Art (A.E.I.O.U.)," by Jim James
"Pets," by Porno for Pyros
"Holocene," by Bon Iver
"In the Anthropocene," by Nick Mulvey and KEYNVOR

To be sure, the list leans dark: a mixtape of cosmic and ecological disaster, delusional exceptionalism, human powers of denial, grief and sorrow, regret and repentance. But there's wonder, too, and even a low, humble kind of hope.

I won't try to explain or justify why each track is in the list. It's nothing so systematic. But I will sometimes bring up one or another of them where it signals, at least for me, some dimension of thought that I am trying but more or less failing to draw out fully.

Like now. I've been haunted for years by the vaguely mournful, dully apologetic "O Children," by Nick Cave and the Bad Seeds. It's a kind of goodbye note from an older generation to their survivors, the children, whom they've left with an awful mess. In a mix of remorse and resignation, Cave asks the children to forgive their elders for what began, naively enough, as a little fun but has become a nightmare that they will be left to inhabit. And now, as the elders depart this gulag of violence, injustice, and degradation, they are leaving the children the keys. It's as if, in the same moment, "we," the older generation, are realizing both the disaster we've left for our children and the fact that it's too late to do much about it.

The older I get, the more "O Children" resonates. I feel the sadness and regret. And I feel a kind of weariness, too—weary of my own inaction, exhausted by my own lack of wholeheartedness, depressed by my own part in our failure of the next generation.

I believe younger people are also weary. But theirs is a weariness infused with frustration, even rage. Sick and tired. This is what I have learned from my college students, and from my own kids, who are now young adults. They have grown up fully aware, and terrified, of the ecological crisis they find themselves in. For many of them, anxiety and climate trauma are a part of everyday life. They have heard the deadlines come and go for the point at which it will be too late to reverse or even significantly slow global warming. They have heard leader after leader of every political and religious stripe promise to address it, and then fail to do so. They do not easily imagine or anticipate grandchildren, let alone great grandchildren, as my generation and earlier ones did. Indeed, many cannot imagine having kids of their own. As one recently told me after class, "I don't want to bring a child into the world when I don't know what is happening and what the future holds. And if humans are to face extinction in the next three hundred years, then my legacy doesn't matter in the grand scheme of cosmic time either."

These young people also recognize the denial that has gotten us to this point. They see it in their own parents and grandparents, not to mention professors. And they worry that, in time, they themselves will learn to practice the same denial.

What to do? Ask for forgiveness and hand them the keys to our broken-down immortality vehicles before we run away? O, children.

REALITY, GRIEF, HOPE

I first tried to write this book as a letter to my own children, and then as a letter to my own students—a kind of long-form version of the Nick Cave song. But that didn't make sense. It's not something I'm telling them or writing *to* them; rather, it's something I've been thinking and talking about *with* them. I want this to be a continuation of those conversations, for which I continue to be grateful and in which I continue to find hope. Indeed, I've come to think of these conversations as our shared *mortality project*—a project that begins not with delusions of godlikeness and human transcendence but with a call to *subscendence*, that is, a call to ground ourselves in our earth creatureliness, to find ourselves in, with, and under the web of interdependence that cradles our being.

My teacher Walter Brueggemann describes the biblical prophets as poets who offer an alternative world to the one offered by the empire.[10] He characterizes this prophetic alternative in terms of a movement from reality to grief to hope. Over against the empire's *ideology* of exceptionalism and special blessing, they expose the *reality* of injustice and exploitation. Over against the empire's suffering- and death-dealing *denial* of real consequences, they give voice to *grief* for human loss and pain. And over against the empire's *despair* when denial no longer holds and it all falls apart, they offer *hope*, which can only be found in the midst of reality and grief.

These three movements, from reality to grief to hope, also give shape to this mortality project: to face the *reality* of human finitude against the delusional *ideology* of godlike human exceptionalism; to *grieve* the irreversible consequences of that ideology over against our widespread *denial*, which leads to even greater oppression, violence, and suffering; and to find new *hope* against the *despair* that the delusion of human exceptionalism ultimately bequeaths to us. I find resources for this kind of hope in returning to the very biblical traditions that have been leveraged in the name of human exceptionalism. I want to crack the Bible's binding and read it again, attending especially to those texts that represent its indigenous religious roots in earth creatureliness, which is in touch with the precarious wonder of human fragility within a larger ecological web of subsistence and interdependence.

Still, for me, this hope must be *palliative*. In healthcare for individuals, a palliative approach is not simply about giving up on the struggle to stay alive. It is about breaking through the denial of death and accepting that death is a normal part of one's life. It's about prioritizing quality of life over quantity of days or years alive. It's about learning to live with necessary pain and suffering, and, at least as importantly, alleviating unnecessary suffering. It's about asking what matters most when one realizes that, barring some kind of miracle, one's time is growing short.

The late Indian Jesuit priest and psychotherapist Anthony de Mello encouraged people to cultivate a spiritual practice imagining ourselves as dead and buried. "I've often said to people that the way to really live is to die. The passport to living is to imagine yourself in your grave. . . . Now look at your problems from that viewpoint. Changes everything, doesn't it? What a lovely, lovely meditation. Do it every day if you have the time. It's unbelievable, but you'll come alive."[11]

I think it's about time for us as a species to do something similar, to imagine our own finitude, our own end, and to have an honest conversation about it. What might a palliative approach to the human future look like? What might it mean to face our collective mortality as part of our story, part of what it means to be human? How, in some cases, might that change our goals and priorities, as individuals and as communities, locally and globally? How, in other cases, might it increase our commitment to present goals and priorities? How is our denial of our collective finitude actually causing more suffering and violence, human and nonhuman, in our communities and in our world? What would it mean, in the face of our collective finitude, to work to alleviate unnecessary suffering, to offer and find forgiveness, to work toward reconciliation, reparation, and justice in our relationships and in our institutions? Whether we have a generation, or seven generations, or even longer, these are questions worth asking.

I

SOON, ALL OF THIS
WILL BE GONE

M Y FIRST JOB after graduate school was at a small liberal arts college in St. Petersburg, Florida. I grew up in Alaska and my wife, Clover, was from the Pacific Northwest, so Florida felt like another planet to us. But the school was a wonderful place to begin our careers, myself as a professor and she as a chaplain. This was the mid-1990s, but it felt like the '60s there. It was the kind of place where classes were as likely to meet on the beach or in a palm-fronded sweat lodge (a senior project turned sacred space on campus) as in the scheduled room, where the smell of weed and patchouli oil were always in the air, and where class guests often included a pet dog or ferret or snake. We loved the school's quirky, free-and-easy sense of community and its dedication to education as transformation and liberation.

During our first year there, I would often bring our four-year-old daughter, Sophie, to class with me. I liked to sit on the table in front of the chalkboard while teaching, and she liked to hunker down underneath it with some crayons and paper, peeking out between my dangling feet at the students while drawing pictures that she would give to anyone who seemed interested at the end of class. Sometimes while we walked back to my office or to a nearby diner for a late breakfast she would comment on the class discussion or tell me about a conversation she had with a student. She was possessed of a disarming sense of assurance about how she saw herself and her surroundings, and she spoke easily and fearlessly from that place. After a class session on religion and gender, she reported that "I told Cyndi that I know I shouldn't like Disney movies because the girl is only happy when she gets saved by the boy, but I like them anyway." After a class on apocalyptic movements, she said, "I told Gunnar that you like to make creepy things interesting."

One typically sunny afternoon, we were driving home from school along a beautiful tree-lined boulevard. Clover and I were in the front of our red Subaru wagon, and Sophie and her baby brother, Seth, were in car seats in the back. We passed a playground in a big public park where kids were swinging and sliding and climbing things while parents watched attentively from nearby park benches. I could see Sophie in the rear-view mirror, happily taking in the huge live oaks, the blue sky, the green grass, the frolicking children.

"Soon," she said, still smiling, "all of this will be gone."

Clover and I glanced at one another as if to ask, "Did she just say what I think she said?"

Perhaps that class session on apocalypticism had shaped her imagination more than I'd realized. Or maybe she had just heard one of our favorite songs, "Pets," by Porno for Pyros, on the car radio, a childlike, happy-go-lucky tune about how we are like the dinosaurs except for the fact that we are bringing about our own demise much faster than they ever could have. But hey, we'll make excellent pets for whoever comes next.

Maybe, but I don't think so. Rather, I think that something in the happiness and simple beauty of the moment awakened along with it a sense, even a vision, of the fleetingness of all that we know and love.

I wonder, do kids have that sense more than we adults do? What if growing up is about learning to forget that uneasy, half-conscious knowledge of the unbearable precariousness of being human in a here-today-gone-tomorrow world? Maybe, over the years, we gradually learn to deny such mortal unease, building moments of experience into a big story, a story of where we've been and where we're going, which provides a kind of narrative bridge to block our view of the abyss we daily cross.

Sophie was right, of course. Everything we were taking in as we drove along that day is now, in a very real sense, "gone." The trees have grown older or died, as have the kids and parents and grandparents. The playground has rusted, broken down, been replaced.

And the Gulf Coast city of St. Petersburg itself could also easily be pretty much "gone" soon enough. Bordered by water on three sides, its highest elevation is a mere forty-four feet above sea level. Much of the city, including that park we were driving past, is not even ten feet above sea level. During our first year there, Sophie had already seen heavy rains turn our neighborhood street and back alley into muddy rivers populated by floating dumpsters, coolers, and palm fronds. She had seen flood waters reach the door handles of our car in the driveway and fill the coin slots of parking meters in the nearby town of St. Pete Beach. When you see flooding like that, even for just a day or two, it is not difficult to imagine water washing the world as we know it away.

"Soon, all of this will be gone."

WHAT IF IT'S ALREADY TOO LATE?

It may not be too late, but it probably is. Not long ago, back in the 1980s, it probably was not. There were opportunities to slow, stop, and perhaps even reverse global warming.[1] There was the 1978 report to the United States Department of Energy by a group of prominent scientists known as the Jasons. They warned that carbon dioxide emissions would be doubled from pre-industrial levels by 2035, raising global temperatures by as much as three degrees Celsius (about 5.4 degrees Fahrenheit). This they believed would cause a rapid melting of the poles, triggering massive forest fires and catastrophic water shortages, turning much of North America into dust bowls.

Then there was the study on climate change by a committee of the National Academy of Sciences, commissioned in 1979 by the Carter administration but not released until 1983 under the Reagan administration. Although the report itself was bleak, largely confirming the Jasons' report and calling for immediate action, the committee's chair and spokesperson, William Nierenberg, along with President Reagan's science advisor, George Keyworth II (best known for promoting the "Star Wars" missile system), played down its urgency and stopped short of making any serious policy changes.

Climate change scientists had long warned that, by the time we had clear signs of the warming effects of carbon dioxide emissions, it would be too late to do anything about them. Then, in 1988, it happened: the hottest summer on Earth in one hundred thirty years of recorded history. In June of that year, Dr. James E. Hansen, director of NASA's Institute for Space Studies, testified before the Senate Energy and Natural Resources Committee that the "greenhouse effect" of global warming, caused by the buildup of carbon dioxide and other gases through human activities, was a reality and would raise temperatures by as much as nine degrees Fahrenheit by 2050, if not sooner. The rate of warming, moreover, would probably not be steady and gradual; widespread deforestation, for example, could speed it up, as dying trees release their stored carbon dioxide into the atmosphere. Senator Timothy E. Wirth of Colorado, who presided over the hearing, said that "the scientific evidence is compelling. . . . Now, the Congress must begin to consider how we are going to slow or halt that warming trend and how we are going to cope with the changes that may already be inevitable."[2]

But even then, in the summer of 1988, more than a third of a century ago, it was not only already inevitable; it was probably already too late to do more than moderately slow the warming trend.[3]

In a matter of decades, coastal cities like St. Petersburg, Miami, Hong Kong, and London could be underwater. The world's ice caps are melting rapidly, many times faster than a hundred years ago, and the sea level is rising. Eventually it will swell more than two hundred feet, swallowing up much of the world's human habitat and raising global temperatures to inhuman highs. No one knows how long that will take—maybe hundreds of years, maybe a couple hundred, maybe by the end of this century.

That's just one of several realistic ways our environment could wash or blow us away. Other plausible scenarios include global pandemics, asteroid showers, and volcanic winters, to name a few.

Not that the world would miss us. It would be just fine without us. Countless plants and animals would continue to thrive and teem. New forms of life would emerge and evolve. A vibrant and diverse post-human world is a very real possibility. Indeed, sooner or later, it is an inevitability. The end of the world as we know it, that is, as a home for human life and society in any form that remotely resembles anything we have known, looms on the horizon.

HUMAN EXCEPTIONALISM

But we have an incredibly hard time imagining such a post-human world. Sure, things are bad. We're trashing our planetary home like it's a battered old frat house. Modest Mouse's song "Lampshades on Fire" is an apt parable of our human situation. It's party time. We're high as kites and glutted from feasting. We barely notice that the lampshades have caught fire. The couch and walls are next. But we'll sober up and get out of here in time, just before the roof falls in and we're all swallowed up in flames. Before this house burns to the ground, the scientists will surely find us an open door to the next one.

In many ways, Octavia Butler's dystopian vision of the mid-2020s in her science fiction novel *The Parable of the Sower*, published in 1993, is proving to be far from fictional: pandemics, fires, water shortages, toxic rain, mass starvation, rampant violence, insufferable poverty, walled communities surviving by isolating themselves from other groups based on class and race, and corporate labor camps promising technological solutions to climate crisis and offering their workers security in exchange for human rights and dignity. But there's one piece of Butler's vision that is not coming true: the real possibility of escaping Earth and finding another planetary home for humankind.

Our apparent inability to imagine our own potential extinction has kept us from making the kinds of radical economic, political, and social changes that would have been necessary to give ourselves a fighting chance at longer-term survival as a species. It's as if we think there's some invisible safety net out there. We may get pretty far down the road to self-destruction, but we'll figure things out in time. We always do. As the hero Mark Watney (played by Matt Damon) puts it in *The Martian*, we'll just have to "science the shit out of this." Which is exactly what he and his NASA colleagues keep doing throughout the movie, all the way to the final scene, in which he explains to his future space-traveling students that, when all hope of survival seems lost, "you can either accept that, or you can get to work. . . . You do the math. You solve one problem and you solve the next one, and then the next. And if you solve enough problems, you get to come home." We can science our way out of anything, we seem to believe.

Why such a failure of imagination when it comes to the very real possibility of a post-human future? We imagine global catastrophes just fine. Stories of asteroid showers, nuclear holocausts, global pandemics, and zombie apocalypses are often the stuff of blockbuster movies. What we cannot seem to imagine, however, is an ending to the story in which we are not saved by some last-minute heroic intervention or escape plan. As our most popular science fiction fantasies attest, we easily imagine us surviving the world, but we cannot imagine the world surviving us.

In their "Imperative to Act," delivered at the 2012 meeting of the United Nations Environmental Programme in Nairobi, Kenya, twenty laureates of the distinguished Blue Planet Prize declared humankind to be in a state of "absolutely unprecedented emergency" in which "society has no choice but to take dramatic action to avert a collapse of civilization." What is keeping us from acting, they said, is not our lack of ingenuity or problem-solving skills, but our lack of recognition of reality, an apparent refusal to understand what is happening. Our extremely rapid evolution in science and technology is matched only by our pathetically slow development of wisdom. "The human ability to do," they write, "has vastly outstripped the ability to understand."[4]

That's true as far as it goes. But what is understanding? Is it simply a rational response to facts? Far from it. Understanding is about seeing how something can be true, how it makes sense, within a particular cultural context and interpretive framework—in other words, a particular hermeneutic.[5] The problem, then, is not simply about doing versus understanding. What we do, and what we don't do, are directly related to our understanding, how we interpret, indeed how we imagine, our world.

I believe that there is something very deeply religious that drives this inability to see and understand our present and future reality: human exceptionalism. At the core of this understanding, this hermeneutic, is a belief in the unique godlikeness of humankind and our entitled dominion over the rest of the natural world—that humans are essentially and fundamentally exceptional to and set apart from nature and its ways, including, above all, death and extinction.[6] This understanding of ourselves and our world serves to turn our attention away from the consequences of our actions.

As we will see, this faith in human exceptionalism has its roots in a form of Christian theology that was invented half a millennium ago to ordain and inspire modern Western capitalism. Built around translations and interpretations of a few biblical verses, this theology proclaims that humans are created uniquely in the image of God and called to "multiply and fill the earth" and to "subdue and have dominion" over it. The early modern philosopher Francis Bacon, for example, called this theology our "charter of foundation" and believed the emerging capitalist order of modern Europe, bringing together technology, science, and economic growth, would be the means by which humankind would finally reclaim our Edenic status of divine dominion over the rest of creation. John Locke used this same biblical idea to justify and ordain the taking of Native American land, which he believed Indigenous peoples forfeited by not fully subduing and maximally using its natural resources.

This same biblically inspired idea of dominion marched into Africa and Asia alongside European explorers and entrepreneurs, justifying imperial expansion, the expropriation of land, and the enslavement of Indigenous peoples, which drove the early, pre-industrial era of so-called mercantile capitalism. Sven Beckert aptly renames this era "war capitalism," highlighting its deep dependence on the military subjugation and extraction of non-Western lands and peoples in order to fuel growth and expansion.[7] This theology of dominion also echoed through the noisy machines and bustling factories of the industrial era, as men of commerce developed new technologies for subduing and harnessing the rest of the natural world, including the labor of other humans. Indeed, this faith in human exceptionalism has often gone hand in hand with European exceptionalism, Christian exceptionalism, American exceptionalism, and white exceptionalism. We will have a lot more to say about that.

Still, aren't we today more enlightened? Haven't we moved beyond such religious fervor? Have we not, over the last century or so, jettisoned these embarrassing religious and theological dimensions of earlier capitalist eras, like booster rockets that are no longer needed as we hurtle upward on our own power?

Quite the contrary. This faith in human exceptionalism, inspired and ordained by a Christian theology of godlike dominion over creation, has only grown in our post-Christian world. Although it has, at least in secular circles, dropped its explicit biblical prooftexts, and even its god, this theology remains the intractable core faith of global capitalism, the religion of the Anthropocene. Detached and floating free from the rest of the Bible and Christianity, it is being fruitful, multiplying, and filling the earth. And in the wake of the death of God, our god-*likeness* has been transformed into self-proclaimed *godhood*. We are the gods now. We can and will science and engineer our way out of any dead end; we can and will transcend our own finitude. Faith in our own godhood, our own divinity, is our ultimate immortality project.

NO TIME FOR LECTURING

It's time for a difficult conversation about our mortality as a species. How did we get to this point? More importantly, what would it be like to live with the understanding that humankind is now in its elder years? Might we, like some of our wiser friends and family members in their twilight years, and like some who face fatal illnesses, ourselves become wiser, discovering ways to live more mindfully and compassionately into our finitude?

For many, our only hope is in the saving power of human ingenuity to invent a way out of the dead end we are approaching and to rediscover an indefinite future with some semblance of the world as we have known it. Of course we can and should hope for that. But such hope very easily slips into unhealthy and ultimately tragic forms of denial. As we will see, this kind of denial, fueled by exceptionalism, often leads to greater violence and unnecessary suffering, as it strives in vain to force reality to conform at any cost. Indeed, the relationship of our shared denial to local and global violence and injustice is a central theme throughout this book.

As I approach three decades as a teacher and a scholar, and as we approach three decades since it was already probably too late to beat or even slow the climate crisis, I find that neither I nor my students, nor the children of my students, consider our current state of frantic denial to be tolerable. I don't pretend to have anything like a fully formed alternative. But I do believe that by asking the questions, as honestly and self-reflectively as we can, and by inviting conversation about those questions, we might find some clarity of understanding, not only about how we got to this latter-day point in human history, but also about where hope now lies—hope not over against grief and loss but in the face of those realities.

During my second year as a professor, some students nominated me to give the school's annual "Last Lecture." A lot of colleges have these. The idea is to address students as if it were going to be your last lecture, as if the end—of your career? your life? the world?—were clearly in view.

I gave it my best shot. Being a religionist and biblical scholar, I imagined myself, tongue-in-cheek, to be a kind of death-bed Moses offering final exhortations to the Israelites who were about to enter the Promised Land without him. I set before them blessings and curses: blessings for pushing the limits of thought and questioning the givens, curses for chasing after the money and settling for easy answers.

It was an okay last lecture. It got a few laughs and gave students a few things to think about. But I could tell that I had mostly disappointed them. They had hoped for something more—more candid, more self-exposing, more ultimate. As if this really were it, my last time with them to talk about what really matters.

Looking back on that time in my life and career, I think I was simply too invested in my own immortality projects, creative ways of denying my own inevitable finitude and mortality, to answer their call. A freshly minted PhD on the ever-rarer tenure track, I was about to publish my first book, which I hoped would transform how everyone thought about gender, ethnicity, and identity politics in the Bible. I was working on a second book and was eagerly pursuing other opportunities to get published and find my voice in the academy and the broader public. I was in hot pursuit, however subconsciously, of immortality, out of touch with mortality and the reality, grief, and hope that can potentially come from such a place.

Those early students of mine are now in their forties. I've stayed in touch with many of them. Some now have children around the age Sophie was when she was sitting under the table drawing pictures for them during class. It won't be long before I could see their kids as students in my classes and their parents at homecomings and commencements.

As far as I'm concerned, this is no time for a last-lecture redux. I've never liked lecturing, even on things I'm called a professor of, let alone on something like this. Nor do I wish to pretend that I am any kind of expert in finding our way in the Anthropocene when time is short. I'm no death doula for the species. But I do want to be part of the growing conversation that seeks to reflect realistically and hopefully on what matters most when time has grown short, which I believe it has. And I join this conversation with those students and their children on my mind and in my heart. Can we set aside, even for a moment or two, our before-it's-too-late urgency in order to ask whether it might already be too late? How did we get here, and what is our path forward? Where do we find hope in light of what really matters, a hope that means something even if, sooner than later, as Sophie once anticipated, "all of this will be gone"?

◆

2

ONCE WE WERE LIKE GODS

H OW DID WE GET HERE? How did we get to the point where
we are on the verge of wearing out our welcome on the planet,
having known decades earlier that such a time would come? And how
can we still be in denial of this reality? What is the genesis of this
delusion of godlike human exceptionalism?

Once upon a time in the West, we believed we were like gods. We
believed that the creator God made humankind only a little lower
than God's very self. And we believed that God blessed and ordained
our species to assume godlike dominion over the rest of creation.

We believed that the Bible told us so: that God created humankind in God's own image. We took this to mean that the creator of
everything, living and nonliving, made us uniquely like him. It was
an image of knowledge and power, omniscient wisdom and omnipo-
tent dominion.

God blessed us and commanded us to go and do and be likewise:
to fill the earth with our species, to conquer and rule over everything
and everyone else. The rest of creation was a limitless storehouse of
God-given resources that existed primarily if not solely for our benefit. It was both our blessing and our responsibility to use this bounty
to the fullest. It was humankind's manifest destiny.

But there was more to the story. God had also created human-kind with free will, that is, with the freedom to choose between right and wrong, good and evil. And with that freedom, we chose to rebel against God by eating the forbidden fruit of the tree of knowledge of good and evil in the Garden of Eden. This is the biblical story of humankind's fall from original godlikeness, from our union with the divine, and our banishment from Paradise.

If you're familiar at all with Christianity, you'll recognize every-thing up to this point as the beginning of a familiar Christian story arc. Perhaps you've heard it in a Lessons and Carols service around Christmastime. Perhaps, like me, you first encountered it in Sun-day school or Vacation Bible School, laid out in scenes on a flan-nelgraph: scene 1, humans created in God's image, bathed in light, surrounded by a worshipfully submissive animal kingdom; scene 2, Adam and Eve in the garden, eating from the tree of knowledge un-der a darkening sky; and scene 3, God banishing the guilty couple from Paradise to make their way as fallen creatures in a mortally threatening world.

This flannelgraph-friendly version of the creation and fall of hu-mankind is based largely on a highly selective synopsis of the first three chapters of the biblical book of Genesis. In fact, it is a mashup of two very different stories of creation. In the first story (Genesis 1:1–2:4a), God makes the world in six days, culminating with human-kind, and creates male and female "in the image of God" and com-mands them to "be fruitful and multiply, fill the earth and subdue it, and have dominion" (1:28). On the seventh day, God rests, taking the first Sabbath. In the second story (Genesis 2:4b–3:24), which imme-diately follows the first, God creates a single human first, before any plants or animals, and then later divides that human into male and female, Adam and Eve. Then comes the story most Christians know as the Fall (Jewish tradition does not read it that way). Eve, in con-versation with the serpent, which Christians often read as Satan in disguise, eats the fruit of the tree of knowledge of good and evil. She then gives it to Adam, who also eats it, no questions asked. Realizing what they've done, God banishes them from Eden, cursing them and their offspring to short lives marked by heavy fieldwork and pain in childbearing.

We will come back to explore these two very different creation stories in detail later. For now, suffice to say that the familiar Christian storyboarding abridges a great deal, melding them together into a single myth of humankind's creation in the image of God, including all the rights and privileges of dominion pertaining thereto, followed by their fall from divine grace and banishment from Paradise into this mortal coil. Which sets the stage in the Christian grand narrative for redemption in and through the saving grace of God in the sacrifice of Jesus Christ.

DOUBLE FALL

The fall, then, according to this familiar Christian synopsis, was twofold: on the one hand, it was a fall from our innocent and pure relationship with our divine creator; on the other hand, it was a fall from our original godlikeness and dominion over the rest of creation. Fallen life outside Paradise does not come easy. Nature often seems to hold dominion over us, as when a mother suffers pain and agony in childbirth, and when the ground bears more thistles than vegetables until the day our dead bodies return to it. The fall was a loss of both divine grace and divine dominion.

In the Christian grand arc, humankind's fall from divine grace through the sin of disobedience is redeemed through Christ, whose sacrifice atones (literally at-ones) for us, reuniting us with God. But what about the second consequence of the fall—our banishment from Paradise and our fall from godlike dominion over creation into a state of suffering and death under the rule of nature?

One traditional answer is that we will transcend our mortality when we die, at which time our immortal souls will finally slough off our mortal flesh and ascend to heaven for all eternity. As an evangelical youth-group kid coming of age in the 1970s and '80s, I knew and lived by this version. I remember these graphic T-shirts that turned ads for popular consumer products into evangelistic messages—like Christian versions of Wacky Packs' fake ads for "Crust" toothpaste and "Weakies, the Breakfast of Chumps." My favorite one was a play on a popular shampoo called Earth Born, which branded itself as a pure and natural alternative to its competitors. Under a cartoonish image of the shampoo bottle with "Earth Born" on the label were written the words " . . . but Heaven bound!" Earth born, but heaven bound.[1] Whereas the shampoo ads were filled with Edenic images of natural harmony, promising to "restore your hair to its original balance," the message of my T-shirt was "Excuse me, and sorry to burst your bubble, but all this is temporary. It's not about getting back to nature or restoring original balance; it's about preparing yourself for what comes after this world."

This broad Christian narrative arc, from dominion to evacuation, lends itself nicely to an understanding of the rest of creation as a stockpile of expendable, ultimately nonrenewable resources. This had to be what God meant when he blessed humankind and told them to subdue and have dominion over the rest of creation. To do anything else would be bad stewardship, rejecting the bounty God had blessed us to take and use.

In Alaska, where I grew up, that meant timber, mining, fishing, and, above all, oil. The Trans-Alaska Pipeline, completed in 1977, carried crude oil across eight hundred miles of wilderness, from Prudhoe Bay on the North Slope to the port town of Valdez. Oil people from Texas, most of them conservative evangelical Christians as far as I could tell, were moving to the "last frontier" in droves to work in the booming energy industry. It was in this environment, with oil gushing and the religious right on the rise, that I first encountered people who believed that God had actually deposited the oil in underground reservoirs at the time of creation so that humans could use it when the time came. There will be exactly as much oil as we will need, they insisted. Refusing to drill for it would be refusing God's bounteous gift.

CHARTER OF FOUNDATION

Enjoying creation's natural resources until it's time to depart our death-bound bodies for heaven is one way to overcome our exile from Paradise and consequent mortality. Still, this interpretation focuses on the denial of one's own *individual* death in the afterlife. The human species, as part of creation, remains decisively mortal, banished from this-worldly Paradise, unable to access the fruit of its tree of life.

In the early modern West, another death-denying workaround gained prominence. While absorbing the common Christian understanding of nonhuman creation ("nature") strictly in terms of use value, as stage and resource for the human drama, this modern version took a different turn, one that provided a firmer foundation for faith in human exceptionalism and godlike dominion in the here and now. It goes like this: Whereas faith in Christ is the path to redemption and reunion with God, thus overcoming the first consequence of the fall, *it is our own human labor in science and industry that will enable us to redeem and realize our original divine blessing and call to subdue and rule over all creation as gods*, to regain Paradise. Faith in Christ overcomes the first consequence of the fall; humankind's own exceptional ingenuity and achievement will overcome the second.

The greatest early advocate and spokesperson for this interpretation of fall and redemption was the philosopher Francis Bacon (1561–1626). A highly influential early proponent of inductive reasoning and scientific methodology, Bacon called the biblical command to fill, subdue, and have dominion over the rest of creation our "charter of foundation" and "the original donation of government" from God.[2] This charter, he believed, ordains and inspires humankind to regain its divine status in the image of its creator God from before the fall, to "recover that right over nature which belongs to it by divine bequest," subjecting the world to human will and benefiting through the marriage of innovative science, technology (what he referred to as the practical or mechanical "arts"), colonial expansion, and economic growth. "For man by the fall fell at the same time from his state of innocence and from his dominion over creation. Both of these losses however can even in this life be in some part repaired; the former by religion and faith, the latter by arts [i.e., technology] and sciences." We were not, by that double fall, "made altogether and forever a rebel."[3] We are called to overcome our fallen state, reclaiming our original godlikeness. This is "the restitution and reinvesting of man to the sovereignty and power . . . which he had in his first state of creation. And to speak plainly and clearly, it is a discovery of all operations and possibilities of operations from immortality (if it were possible) to the meanest mechanical practice."[4] Such, indeed, is God's will for us.

As historian of science Evelyn Fox Keller and others have shown, Bacon's vision of the restitution of global dominion through science and technology was aggressively patriarchal and sexist, representing nature as a woman whom the (male) scientist must sexually subdue, objectify, and control. "It is Nature herself," Keller writes, "who is to be the bride, who requires taming, shaping, and subduing by the scientific mind."[5] As if offering fatherly advice to a son, Bacon writes, "I am come in very truth leading to you Nature with all her children to bind her to your service and make her your slave. . . . My dear, dear boy, what I plan for you is to unite you with things themselves in a chaste, holy and legal wedlock. And from this association you will secure an increase beyond all the hopes and prayers of ordinary marriages, to wit, a blessed race of Heroes and Supermen."[6] The restoration of Paradise envisioned here imagines science as male subject and the rest of creation as his female object, whom he is commanded to subdue and have dominion over in order to recover Paradise, filling the earth with "a blessed race" of godlike superheroes.

There are, of course, many other ways to read the biblical dominion verse, especially, as we will see, when it is tempered with and counterposed against other biblical texts. But biblical images and stories rarely stay put within their canonical contexts; they tend to detach and circulate on their own, attaching to other ideas and movements on very different horizons of meaning. So it is with the dominion verse. It has taken on a life of its own as a kind of meme in story form, a highly condensed, extremely durable, and easily portable myth that has replicated and embedded itself in the larger cultural gene pool.[7]

This little story-shaped meme of godlike dominion captured the heart and soul of the modern West over half a millennium ago and has carried it for centuries. Scientists, explorers, philosophers, artists, and religious and political leaders believed that they were realizing their own God-given divinity in the world through the subjection of all of nature to their godlike dominion and control. Indeed, failing to carry this mission forward to multiply, fill, subdue, and dominate creation would have been an outright act of disobedience against God. As the well-known English civic leader and theologian John William Fletcher put it, the dominion verse "is the original grant of Power . . . and whosoever wantonly resisteth the power which Providence calls him to obey, breaks this great political charter of God."[8]

Still, this grant of power was apparently not available to everyone. Many humans—especially non-Christian humans, non-European humans, and female humans, which is to say the huge majority of humans—were projected by its white European male grantees as closer to nature than to the image of God and therefore belonging under their dominion. The "primitive" cultures and "heathen" theologies of other peoples were dismissed for their intimate dependence on their natural environments and their beliefs that divinity resided not only in humans but also in nonhuman animals and things.

The late seventeenth-century political philosopher John Locke (1632–1704), intellectual patron saint of the founders of the United States, for example, used the dominion verse to justify colonizing Native American land. In his doctrine of the natural human right to possess private property, he argued that labor invests ownership in land. To work the land and make it be fruitful, as God commanded, is to lay claim to it.

> His labour hath taken it out of the hands of nature, where it was common, and belonged equally to all her children, and hath thereby appropriated it to himself. . . . He by his labour does, as it

were, enclose it from the common. . . . God and his reason commanded him to subdue the earth—i.e., improve it for the benefit
of life and therein lay out something upon it that was his own, his
labour. He that, in obedience to this command of God, subdued,
tilled, and sowed any part of it, thereby annexed to it something
that was his property.[9]

According to Locke's doctrine, the Native Americans appeared to
be failing to take full advantage of the land as resource, through their
labor. They had "left to nature" the "wild woods and uncultivated
waste of America," thereby forfeiting their claim to it.

The biblical theology of godlike dominion likewise ordained the
West's violent military dominion over non-Western lands, natural resources, and peoples that made possible the rise of industrial capitalism. The idea that capitalism became the dominant economic system
by means of technological revolutions in mechanization obscures the
truth of its roots in exploitation and violence. Before the rise of industrial capitalism in the late seventeenth and early eighteenth centuries,
there was a crucial period of what Beckert calls "war capitalism," which
was built on "the violent expropriation of land and labor in Africa and
the Americas. From these expropriations came great wealth and new
knowledge, and these in turn strengthened European institutions and
states—all crucial preconditions for Europe's extraordinary economic
development by the nineteenth century and beyond."[10]

War capitalism also coincided and interacted with another development in sixteenth-century Europe, what Gary Snyder describes as
ecological impoverishment, a denial of the inherent value of the nonhuman world. Europeans "were rapidly becoming nature-illiterate,"
as most indigenous vegetation had been lost to agriculture. Those
growing up in this context "had less chance to learn how wild systems
work." This newly wild-illiterate modern European culture "denied
first soul, then consciousness, and finally even sentience to the natural world. Huge numbers of Europeans, in the climate of a nature-
denying mechanistic ideology, were losing the opportunity for direct

experience of nature," further enabling its objectification as a store of resources whose value is based on utility.[11]

Thus the non-Western and the wild, seen as uncultured and un-cultivated, were modernity's twin others. Indeed they were often pro-jected as one and the same: non-European peoples and cultures were seen as uncivilized insofar as they were seen as with wild nature, even as wild nature was often identified as a foreign threat to Western civ-ilization and economic development.

Capitalism was never innocent, never simply a liberal faith in free markets. Nor was it ever simply Western. Depending from its incep-tion on colonial expansion, the expropriation of land, and slavery, it has always been global, and it has always relied on violent domina-tion. It was a remaking of the world with an inside and an outside: the inside was the "civilized" West, with its free markets, its noble "spirit of capitalism," and its enlightenment; and the outside was the global network of colonized, expropriated, and enslaved continents, Asia, Africa, and the Americas, where the inherent violence of war capitalism was constantly at work. Scientific exploration and discov-ery on the inside went hand in hand with imperial exploration and extraction on the outside. Enlightenment inside, violence outside.

The dominion delusion was at work on both the inside and the outside, driving both the enlightenment on the inside and colonial-ism on the outside. Capitalism's early networks of trade were always at the same time missionary networks of Christendom, and the modern biblical vision of dominion that drove both treated non-Christian peoples less as fellow human beings and more as part of the natural world that called for subjection, religiously and economically. Thus the subjection of nature and the subjection of other peoples and lands went hand in hand, the former representing capitalism's European inside and the latter representing capitalism's subaltern outside.

This biblically inspired dominionism continued to reverberate through the noisy machines and bustling factories of the industrial era, as men of commerce developed new technologies for subduing and harnessing nature. Echoes of the dominion verse ring loudly in speeches, sermons, and business journals of the nineteenth century: James Watts's combustion engine subdues heat particles; God created animals as living beings instead of as slabs of meat so that they could be kept fresh until their time for the slaughterhouse; horse poop smells more pleasant than other animal poops because God knew their use value would be in close proximity to humans.

This spirited proclamation from Samuel Martin's popular 1851 lecture, "The Instincts of Industry," is typical of the exuberant embrace of industrial capitalist faith in biblical dominion:

> All terrestrial things come to man and ask him for employment. The Gases touch us and bid us feel after them. The Metals lie under our feet in perfect vassalage. The Air whispers—"May I serve you?" The Lightning just shews itself and retires—but it leaves on the heavens the inscription—"Electricity was made for man." The Sea rolls up to our feet and asks to be our burden-bearer. The River runs up and down like a Vehicle with noiseless and everlasting wheels—plying for Hire. The Trees of the forest lift up their heads and flowers wear bright raiment that they may not be overlooked, but that we may be ministered unto by them in the order of their course. Birds and Beasts, Fish and Reptiles, come to us that we may name some service within their sphere. The many-voiced Earth utters this one cry in the ear of man—"Let me be your servant." . . . And when men catch and imprison and employ the vagrant and subtile Gas—when men mould the massive metals—when they move among the Animal and Vegetable Creation as Lords—then do they fulfil one part of their mission. What a multitude of subjects belong to the Empire which Industry is commissioned to subdue! . . . to sum up all—when we get at the secrets of Nature and expound them—when we lay hold of the powers of Nature and employ them—when we take possession of the riches of Nature and dispose of them . . . then Man is obedient to the primitive commission—HAVE DOMINION OVER THE EARTH AND SUBDUE IT.[12]

Here creation itself is imagined as a giant labor factory built by the modern god-men of industry according to the biblical charter of foundation. "Made for man," nonhuman beings are meaningless apart from their human use value. They are all essentially machines for human advancement.[13] Each one comes to him, begging for a job, or rather to be enslaved. "Let me be your servant," the chorus of nature cries. Catch, imprison, and employ me, please! In light of associations of non-European peoples with nonhuman nature, his descriptions of these different natural entities—rivers, plants, animals, elements—as foreigners to be captured and enslaved is telling of the continued othering of non-white, non-male peoples as "terrestrial things" alongside the rest of nonhuman nature.

CHOSENNESS AND VIOLENCE

It is not difficult to see how faith in this highly selective form of (modern, Western European, male) human exceptionalism and special blessing relates to another biblical theme, namely, chosenness.

In biblical narrative, the people of Israel, the descendants of Abraham and Sarah, are God's chosen ones, blessed and commanded to become a great nation. Divine chosenness is the basis for the violent displacement of the inhabitants of Canaan, and the expropriation of that land as their "promised land." Later, during the rebuilding of Jerusalem after the Babylonian exile, chosenness is also the basis for the ethnic cleansing of God's chosen people by removing from the community all those foreigners who had married into it, along with their children.

Then there is Christian chosenness. This claim to chosenness is based on supersessionism, the belief that, by rejecting Christ, Israel forfeited its chosenness, which has now been transferred to the church, whose adherents have superseded Israel as the new heirs of divine blessing and promise. This ideology inspired and continues to underwrite the long, bloody history of anti-Judaism and anti-Semitism, which is driven above all by Christian insecurity about its claims to chosenness.

Then there is American chosenness, which is built on the belief that the United States is a Christian nation, the new Israel, chosen by God to be the leader of all the nations, who will be blessed through it. This is the founding myth of the United States. Every successful political leader professes faith in it, or pretends to. It is, moreover, the ground and inspiration for westward expansion, the displacement of Indigenous populations (imagined as the new Canaanites), and the expropriation of their native lands. It also underwrites and inspires American expansion and exploitation around the world, usually in the name of spreading democracy and free market capitalism.

In his essay "Choosing Against Chosenness," Walter Brueggemann shows how these biblically inspired assertions of chosenness, especially the Christian and American versions, are also inextricably linked to white supremacism as an assertion of white chosenness:

> The rather inchoate but pervasive appeal to chosenness in the public rhetoric of the United States has within it an unexpressed but powerful element of white chosenness, so that the theme of "chosenness" can also be a place-holder for racism. There is no doubt that American chosenness derives especially from European antecedents, so that the "real Americans" who are chosen are those with European rootage. Much of the rhetoric of US chosenness is also marked by a hostility to "foreigners" (nonwhites) who, it is said, diminish chosenness, and by "Christian" rhetoric of "taking back our country" from the foreigners and restoring it to proper order and management. Much of the great triumphal language of the church easily imagined white missionaries carrying the gospel to benighted nonwhites.[14]

From Israelite chosenness to Christian chosenness to American chosenness to white chosenness, each building on the next. Brueggemann shows, moreover, how these four interrelated claims to chosenness invariably express themselves in three characteristic ways, which together lead inevitably to violence.

First, chosenness manifests itself in *entitlement*, that is, special status imputed by God that cannot otherwise be earned or merited on account of one's own efforts. Israel is promised the land as an entitlement. The Christian church claims to be entitled to a special, saving intimacy with God through Christ. America claims entitlement to limitless freedom, land, and resources. And white people claim entitlement to a wealth of social and material "blessings," from housing to education to healthcare, which they may choose to hand down to those who are unentitled and underprivileged—"less blessed," as some say.

Second, chosenness manifests itself in *exclusion*. The only way for chosenness to mean anything is if others are not chosen. "We" exclude "them" as an anxious assertion of our chosenness. The Israelites exclude the Canaanites as foreign "others," threats to the purity of their singular chosenness, when in fact we know from historical research that the two peoples were closely related culturally and linguistically, not to mention largely indistinguishable in the archeological record of ancient cultures in the southern Levant region (modern-day Israel, Palestine, and Jordan). Christians exclude the people of other religions, including Jews whom they claim to supersede, from the grace of God, warning the faithful not to be swayed from their faith by unbelievers. Americans exclude more recent and would-be immigrants as well as Indigenous peoples. And white American racist exclusion is pervasive but nowhere more blatant than in longstanding practices of segregation, whether or not "separate but equal," before and after such practices were judged to be illegal.

Third, chosenness manifests itself in *extraction*. In Hebrew biblical narrative, the twelve tribes of Israel, led by Joshua, extract the land of Canaan, which was promised to Abraham, Sarah, and their descendants as God's chosen people. Christian Europeans, also laying claim to God's favor, believed they were chosen to extract the lands, resources, and people of Africa, Asia, and the Americas. The United States, too, believed it was chosen to extract native lands, including their oil, timber, and other natural "resources," and to extract nonwhite life through slavery and cheap labor. Indeed, European and American colonizers drew inspiration from the ancient biblical conquest narratives, boldly proclaiming themselves to be God's new chosen people, destined to dislocate Indigenous populations in order to take possession of new promised lands.[15]

Another word for chosenness in the context of this dominionist theological arc is, of course, *exceptionalism*—the assertion of being exceptional to and excepted from the rest.[16] Such exceptionalisms are never secure because they are always delusional, idealizations and deifications of ourselves at our fantasy best, images of the infinite wisdom and death-defying dominion we long for. They are immortality vehicles, denying our finitude and interdependence. And like all forms of denial, they inevitably issue in more violence, pressing down and away all that we need to believe is "other," the unentitled, excluded, extracted "them."

WISH FULFILLMENT

In his critique of Christian religion, the nineteenth-century German philosopher Ludwig Feuerbach famously declared that "God is man writ large." Meaning that the Christian idea of God is in fact a projection of an idealized image of the human, indeed the male human. Humankind, Feuerbach argued, has created God in our own image and then dialed up all his powers of intelligence and strength to eleven—that than which nothing greater can humanly be conceived, to borrow from Saint Anselm in a way that he probably wouldn't appreciate. "God is man's highest feeling of self," Feuerbach wrote, "free from all contrarities, or disagreeables. . . . God is man's highest feeling of freedom."[17]

When Freud declared religion to be an illusion, he was saying something very similar. An illusion is something that we very much wish to be true. It is, in other words, a form of wish fulfillment. When we are children, at least in an ideal world, our parents help us feel safe and secure, distracting us from the brutal realities of human and natural violence, suffering, and death all around. As we grow older and lose our faith in that parental sheltering, religion steps in to provide the illusory security and safety that we so desperately wish were real and true. Religion, then, is a form of wish fulfillment, an entirely understandable illusion.

Whether or not you agree with Freud that all religion is always illusory in this sense, I would argue that the biblically inspired modern myth of godlike dominion and human exceptionalism is. The raging insecurity and fragility that drive it, as well as its cascading claims to chosenness, hide just beneath its surface.

We tend to imagine the rise of modernity as a kind of creation *ex nihilo*, born purely of the ideas of great minds. But the truth is that it was born out of and over against chaos. Europe during the sixteenth and seventeenth centuries was overwhelmed with social, political, and religious turmoil. It was being tossed to and fro by religious conflicts, assassinations and executions, the Thirty Years War, and other crises. As philosopher Stephen Toulmin makes profoundly clear, it was against this horrific backdrop that modern scientists and philosophers sought to establish a rational order for society that would parallel the order and nature of God. Toulmin calls this new vision "cosmopolis," that is, a *polis* or political order that mirrors and corresponds with the divinely established order of creation, the *cosmos*. This vision of cosmopolis was not only social and economic, therefore, but also deeply religious. It was an attempt to establish cosmic and social order against the flood waters that threatened to overcome it.[18]

No wonder that the dominionist image of godlike human subjugation of all things rose to the theological surface again and again. It is modernity's origin story, establishing social, political, and cosmic order against chaos, creating a sacred cosmopolis against a world otherwise prone to helter-skelter. And its main tenet of faith is human exceptionalism, the belief that the human species is exceptional to the rest of creation, whose ultimate end is extinction. That humankind's signature is God writ small.

However much good and bad this faith has produced—however much violence and suffering, however much thriving and happiness—it was and is founded on a theology of wish fulfillment, born of and driven by deep and abiding insecurities about our all-too-human unexceptionalness.

3

WE ARE THE GODS NOW

ONCE WE BELIEVED we were *like* God, created in God's image, blessed and charged to fill, subdue, and rule over the rest of creation. And although we had fallen from our original state and been exiled from Paradise by that same God, our exile was not necessarily permanent. We had the power within us to regain and restore ourselves, realizing our highest potential for dominion, as God had originally intended. That was our charter of foundation, the founding myth of our godlike human exceptionalism.

But look a little more closely into that story. There's more: the potential to be not only *like* God but to *be* gods, even to replace the creator God altogether.

"Look," God said after Eve and Adam had eaten from the tree of knowledge, "the human is like one of us, knowing good and evil. Now, lest he send forth his hand and take also from the tree of life and eat and live forever . . ." (Genesis 3:22).[1] To prevent that from happening, God immediately sends them out of Eden, far from the tree of life.

"The human has become like one of us." That is what provokes God to kick them out of the Garden of Eden. The last time God spoke in the first-person plural, in the first creation story, being like God seemed to be the divine intention: "Let us make humans in our image" (Genesis 1:26). Here, however, God is apparently concerned that they have gotten *too* close. Perhaps it is this blurring of the divine-human line that makes God slip oddly into "we" language. At any rate, God decides to put some distance between them.

Apparently, the biblical recipe for divinity is a fruit cocktail from two forbidden trees: the tree of knowledge and the tree of life. Knowledge (including self-knowledge or self-consciousness) plus immortality is what the creator God has, and what humans could also have if they eat from both trees. God does not want that. In the serpent's conversation with Eve before she decided to eat fruit from the tree of knowledge, he told Eve that it was not forbidden because it would kill her, as she believed, but because God was worried it would make her become like God. It turns out the serpent was right. And if the humans were to become gods, they would no longer need this God or any other beyond themselves.

Once we notice this divine insecurity in the story, it is not a big leap to imagine a new day for humankind, after religion, after God. A day when humans have superseded and replaced this God. When we are the gods.

This is what Feuerbach meant when he said that the seed of Christianity's undoing is within itself. That seed is the insistence on worshipping a God that is an idealized, writ-large image of ourselves. "God is man, man is God; it is not I, but religion that denies the God who is *not* man." Atheism, he therefore declared, is the "secret truth" of Christianity, which, "in its heart, in its essence, believes in nothing else than the truth and divinity of human nature."[2]

Influenced by Feuerbach, Friedrich Nietzsche famously read this biblical story of the "fall" in just such a way, as "the story of God's hellish fear of science."[3] It is an early anticipation of the fall of God from divinity and the replacement of that God by humankind through its own scientific advancement. To be sure, Nietzsche believed we were far from realizing that potential. We would continue to live in caves, he speculated, worshipping this God's shadow, for thousands more years.

WE ARE THE GODS NOW   ◆   43

UNDERSTANDING OUR DIVINITY

These days it's clearer than it ever could have been to Nietzsche that we won't have thousands of years, or even a thousand. Perhaps that's why, in the middle of the twentieth century, in the near wake of two world wars, the Holocaust, and the bombings of Hiroshima and Nagasaki, and at the dawn of the Great Acceleration and the Anthropocene, we found ourselves proclaiming with increasing frequency and conviction not only that God was dead but also that humankind had succeeded him. Just as we were beginning to realize the real potential for modern science and technology to bring mass death, even extinction, we began to proclaim our early arrival to divinity.

Some saw in all that mass anthropogenic self-annihilation an early lesson in godhood: while we have begun to realize our divine *power*, including the potential to destroy ourselves, we have yet to take on divine *responsibility*.

Echoing and confirming the serpent's prediction and God's worry in Genesis that humans have "become as gods," Stuart Brand introduced the first issue of his *Whole Earth Catalog* in 1968 with this pronouncement: "We *are* as gods and might as well get used to it."[4] The *Whole Earth Catalog*, which Apple cofounder Steve Jobs called "the Bible of my generation," meant to provide the tools for individuals to realize our divine power and responsibility outside the controls of government, big business, education systems, and institutional religion. Brand's call to take up our divinity was in this sense a critique of institutional failures and a turn to grassroots experimentation with tools both old and new. At the same time, his "might as well" makes his proclamation sound a little flippant. Granted, we didn't exactly choose to be gods, and we're not really sure we want to be. But here we are anyway, gods. The old gods that we used to rely on are gone, and our institutions are failing us. So, what the hell, let's see if we can get used to our new divine status—maybe we can even get good at it. We might as well give it a try.

Brand later acknowledged that his call for humankind to assume its divinity was inspired by a similar call a year earlier by social anthropologist Sir Edmund Leach in his famous Reith Lectures, entitled *A Runaway World*, which first aired on BBC Radio in 1967. "Men have become like gods," Leach began. "Isn't it about time that we understood our divinity? Science offers us total mastery over our environment and over our destiny, yet instead of rejoicing we feel deeply afraid. Why should this be?"[5]

The problem, as Leach saw it, was that we had thus far refused to embrace our own divinity. Most of us, he said, remain passive spectators. On the one hand, we watch in awe as scientists reveal deeper and deeper complexities in our natural world. On the other hand, we watch in dread as new technologies risk bringing about catastrophes beyond our ability to contain or control them. At the same time, "The scientist sees himself as explorer, not as creator. He takes it for granted that we must accept the rules of nature as we find them. He refuses to act 'like a god.'" Thus, Leach believed, we are missing the opportunities—and the responsibilities—of our divinity. Science is not restricted to describing and explaining the way things are now. On the contrary, science is our means of participating in the evolution of nature and thus determining our future. "Even the wildest fancies of science fiction are not far removed from possibility. If we so chose we could participate in the processes of nature in a quite unprecedented way and fashion a world to suit our own convenience."[6] Our capacity to overcome our own mortal limitations and sufferings is hindered only by our reluctance to accept and act fully on our own divinity.

TRANSCENDING OUR WETWARE

These early proclamations of our newfound divinity and apparent reluctance to accept it point to a deep cultural ambivalence that continues to this day. On the one hand, they exalt our potential to realize a thriving divine dominion, to create our own reality, and ultimately to overcome human suffering, death, and extinction. They herald a horizon of infinite possibility. They imagine divinely procreative

power for humankind. On the other hand, they call out a deep un-
ease about that potential. Whether we express these ideas passively
(Leach) or half-heartedly (Brand), we seem reluctant about them.
And this reluctance belies our lack of faith in our own divinity.

The same ambivalence, between attraction and fear, between exuberant embrace of and lack of faith in human godhood, is prevalent
to this day.[7] News and popular media are filled with warnings about
the dangers of our divine aspirations, especially concerning the latest
advances in artificial intelligence and robotics. These warnings echo
familiar horror scripts, from *Frankenstein* to *Blade Runner* to *Westworld*, about what inevitably goes wrong when humans play at being
creator gods, making machines in our image, or remaking ourselves
in the image of machines. The lesson inevitably recalls the biblical
story of the fall: our aspirations to divinity, however fortified by the
fruits of new knowledge, will end in suffering, exile, and early death.

Still, many today embrace the call to realize godhood. Indeed,
their faith in our potential to transcend the human condition are
often proclaimed with evangelistic zeal. Most of them are part of a
movement best known as transhumanism, which aims to use new
and emerging technologies to overcome or transcend humankind's
biological limitations. Most often this means somehow extracting the
potentially immortal contents and processes of the conscious mind
from the tragically short-lived flesh-and-blood wetware that currently
hosts it.[8] Some, for example, are working on "whole brain emulation,"
the modest goal of which is to convert the human mind into a computational model that could then be transferred from a human body,
bound as it is to decay and death, into other, more durable vehicles.
Others are working on infinitely extending our human lifespans in
the bodies we already have, or ones very like them. And if that possibility seems too far off in the future for me to make it, I can have
myself—or, more practically and cheaply, just my brain—cryogeni-
cally frozen and stored until the opportunity for resurrection arrives.

A core conviction of transhumanism is that there is no distinction
between nature and technology, between the born and the made. It's

all nature. We are symbiotic with technology, and we always have been. The difference now, many transhumanists would say, is that we are becoming conscious of our potential to take control, to upgrade ourselves and our environment. It is time to do what Edmund Leach was essentially calling for half a century ago: to "participate in the processes of nature in a quite unprecedented way and fashion a world to suit our own convenience."

In 1999, the futurist philosopher Max More wrote "A Letter to Mother Nature," which has become something of a manifesto for the movement.[9] "Sorry to disturb you," the letter begins, "but we humans—your offspring—come to you with some things to say. (Perhaps you could pass this on to Father, since we never seem to see him around.)" More first thanks her for all the wonderful qualities with which she has bestowed us by means of her "slow but massive, distributed intelligence." These include a lifespan much longer than most other animals'; a complex brain capable of language, reason, creativity, self-awareness, and empathy; and "free rein of the planet." And yet, all these gifts notwithstanding,

> you have in many ways done a poor job with the human constitution. You have made us vulnerable to disease and damage. You compel us to age and die—just as we're beginning to attain wisdom. You were miserly in the extent to which you gave us awareness of our somatic, cognitive, and emotional processes. You held out on us by giving the sharpest senses to other animals. You made us functional only under narrow environmental conditions. You gave us limited memory, poor impulse control, and tribalistic, xenophobic urges. And, you forgot to give us the operating manual for ourselves!

In other words, we want, well, more. Therefore, on behalf of humankind, More respectfully submits our declaration of independence from nature in the form of seven amendments. First, "We will no longer tolerate the tyranny of aging and death." By whatever

technological means necessary, from gene therapy to synthetic or-
gans, every individual will be able to live as long as they want.

Second, "We will expand our perceptual range through biotechnological and computational means." We will exceed the limits of the
five senses themselves, inventing new senses of perception to enlarge
our experience and understanding of the world around us.

Third, "We will improve on our neural organization and capacity," extending our intellectual capacities for computation, reason,
and memory.

Fourth, "We will supplement the neocortex with a 'metabrain,'"
that is, a distributed computational network into which individuals
will integrate their own minds in order to improve self-awareness and
better manage emotions.

Fifth, "We will no longer be slaves to our genes." We will take
control of our genetic programming, revising unwanted evolutionary
accidents and fixing individual or species defects.

Sixth, "We will cautiously yet boldly reshape our motivational
patterns and emotional responses in ways we, as individuals, deem
healthy." We will temper and refine our emotions, trimming excesses
and curtailing dogmatisms, thereby becoming more reasonable and
rational.

Seventh and finally, "We will not limit our physical, intellectual, or
emotional capacities by remaining purely biological organisms." With
all due respect to our carbon-based composition, we will take over our
own biochemistry, developing new compounds while also integrating
new technologies into our biotechnological human-machine selves.

Here, then, is a polite yet forceful and supremely confident declaration of independence from subjection to the laws and limits of
nature, above all to mortality. It is an expression par excellence of
human exceptionalism, excepting our species from the rest of nature
by means of our own exceptional potential to transcend it.

More's parenthetical joke about our absent Father God notwithstanding, it is clear that the Mother Nature to whom the letter is
addressed is essentially standing in for what we used to know as the

biblical creator God. Far from a simple personification of the unintentional forces of evolution, this Mother Nature is described as a beneficent creator. Her creation has unfolded according to her design and providence, however slow and massively distributed. But now her human children are all grown up, and it's time to claim our own agency, indeed sovereignty, indeed divinity. It is time for us to pick up where she has mostly left off. Now we are our own creators, designer gods of our own nature and destiny.

One of transhumanism's most zealous evangelists is the Emmy-winning filmmaker and futurist philosopher Jason Silva. In his popular lecture and video "We Are the Gods Now," Silva enthusiastically makes the case that we humans are on the cusp of creatively engineering our way out of the human condition of finitude and death and assuming our divinity.

> The creative solution to the problem of death, I think, is the engineering solution. It's the way through which we remake the world. It's the way in which we transcend our limitations, using science and technology. . . . We transcend time, space and distance. Technology is our extended phenotype. . . . It's really what we are. Our skyscrapers, our jet engines—that's us . . . we are on our way to becoming gods.[10]

Central here is the idea that technology is not only a means of living beyond our embodied human limitations but also a means of *transcending* them, ultimately achieving godhood. "Through technology," he says, "we transcend the limitations of thought, reach and vision. We extend ourselves . . . we punch a few buttons and we send our thoughts through time and space, transcending time, space, distance. We're gods."

As Marshall McLuhan famously argued over half a century ago, technologies are extensions of ourselves that fundamentally alter what it means to be human. We create new technologies, and then they create us in new ways.[11] Technology extends our bodily perceptions and experiences in and of the world. Our phones, watches, and implants connect us with webs and clouds of information and processing power that are beyond our individual cognitive capacities and affordances. Robotic devices and other technologies integrate with our biological bodies to extend and overcome limitations in our neuromuscular, cardiovascular, and sensory powers. Jet engines extend our landlocked bodies all over the planet and into outer space. Iron extends our embodied limits of teeth and fingernails for killing and eating. Earthenware pots extend our bodily limits for holding water and therefore staying hydrated. And so on, all for better and/or worse.

For Silva and others, however, technology's potential to *extend* beyond the limits of our human condition is actually the means of *transcending* those limits, achieving a fundamental, categorical change in us that will solve the problem of death and finitude. Technology is our immortality vehicle.

MYSTICISM EX MACHINA

As our biotechnological evolution continues to accelerate exponentially, we will, very soon, realize a kind of tipping point in what it means to be human. There will be an ontological epiphany of a new kind of human being who transcends the limits that have been ours since the beginning.

This moment of transcendence is one way of describing what inventor and futurist philosopher Ray Kurzweil calls the Singularity. In his best-selling *The Singularity Is Near: When Humans Transcend Biology*, he defines the Singularity as

> a future period during which the pace of technological change will be so rapid, its impact so deep, that human life will be irreversibly transformed. Although neither utopian nor dystopian, this epoch will transform the concepts that we rely on to give meaning to our lives, from our business models to the cycle of human life, including death itself.[12]

The Singularity is near, according to Kurzweil, on account of what he calls "the law of accelerating returns." This law states that evolution, which is now technological as well as biological, is accelerating at an exponential rate. It is now a matter of decades before "information-based technologies will encompass all human knowledge and proficiency," including intellectual, emotional, and moral capacities.[13] This radical transformation, this extension, will be the transcendence of our frail "version 1.0 biological bodies." Of our biological brains, too: "We will fully understand human thinking and will vastly extend and expand its reach. By the end of this century, the nonbiological portion of our intelligence will be trillions of trillions of times more powerful than unaided human intelligence."[14]

Kurzweil's Singularity is a far cry from Max More's vision of human individuals engineering their independence from Mother Nature as smarter, faster, more rational and moral immortals. "If you wonder what will remain unequivocally human in such a world," Kurzweil writes, "it's simply *this quality:* ours is the species that inherently seeks to extend its physical and mental reach beyond current limitations."[15] Humankind's unique contribution to the Singularity will be, in the end (which is only the beginning), a general quality, namely, our desire to transcend our mortal selves. When we do so, will we as individuals somehow also make it intact, as individual conscious minds, albeit disembodied? It doesn't sound like it. I'm reminded of the climactic scene at the end of the second season of the television series *Westworld*, in which row after row of the AI hosts hurtle their robotic bodies through a giant electronic threshold and into "the Valley Beyond," losing themselves in a heavenly scene of disembodied collective consciousness.

If Silva is among transhumanism's most zealous evangelists, then Kurzweil is among its most serious theologians. Indeed, Kurzweil is not averse to representing his vision of human transcendence via the Singularity in explicitly religious terms. In an online conversation with "Molly 2004," transcribed in his book, the question of whether God exists quickly becomes the question of whether the universe exists, and whether Kurzweil believes in it. He says he does, by a "leap of faith." All he can know for certain, he says in true Cartesian spirit, are his thoughts. When Molly 2004 asks whether he thinks the universe has consciousness, as most religious people believe God does, Kurzweil answers, "The universe is not conscious—yet. But it will be. Strictly speaking, we should say that very little of it is conscious today. But that will change and soon," at which point the universe will awaken and very quickly become "sublimely intelligent."[16] This universe, awakened as the Singularity, which is the fulfillment of biological and technological evolution, will be the *mysterium* into which we humans will ultimately lose ourselves.

As a religionist, I do not hesitate to characterize Kurzweil's vision of human transcendence in the Singularity as a kind of religious mysticism. His is a vision of ego transcendence through ego annihilation, in which human individuality and selfhood are ultimately lost in universal, all-encompassing, infinite mystery. As Mark O'Connell aptly puts it, Kurzweil is "a conduit for the mysteries of technology, a prophet of a world to come, in which an infinite and instrumental intelligence will finally release us from the burden of our humanity." His is a vision of "a kind of computational pantheism" soon to be realized.[17]

In this light, the Singularity is not so much a solution to the problem of death as it is a mystical vision of a post-human humankind, in which biological humans, in all their self-conscious individuality and particularity, are sacrificed up to an infinitely larger, universal intelligence. Such a vision stands apart from many more popular utopian images of better, faster, smarter biomechanical human beings, no longer subject to mortality and finitude. Kurzweil's transhuman mysterium is also ultimately a post-human mysterium, a transcendence of biology by means of dying to oneself.

I find myself compelled by some dimensions of transhumanism. Not only do I agree intellectually, but I resonate personally, with its basic anthropological starting point: we humans are not standalone, discrete individuals, contained and isolated within the "ancient biological skin-bag," as Andy Clark puts it.[18] We are intersubjective beings who extend into the world through technologies, from neo-lithic grinding stones to robotic arms, from shofars to iPhones. We extend and connect across time and space with other beings, human and nonhuman, animate and inanimate. There is a transhumanness to being human.

Yet such transhuman extensions beyond our mortal bodies are not entirely or even mostly within our control. They cannot be engineered. They exceed our conscious goals and intentions, our best-laid plans. And this reality points to what is most problematic about so much of the transhumanist movement: its fundamental distinction between mind and body, spirit and matter, and its faith in the sovereignty of mind and spirit over body and matter. As many of its proponents put it, the mind is the code, the operating system. It could live forever if it weren't for its tragically fragile and perishable hardware of flesh and bone, bound to return to the ground from which it came.

O'Connell, along with John Gray and others, rightly recognize in transhumanism's mind-over-body, spirit-over-flesh dichotomy a kinship with the early Christian religion of Gnosticism, which proclaimed salvation from the material world through special knowledge, or *gnosis*.[19] Later rejected as heretical by what eventually became orthodox Roman Christianity, Gnosticism viewed the human soul or mind as one's true immaterial essence and the only means through which one can access divinity. The body, along with the rest of the material world, entraps and encases the soul, potentially preventing it from its spiritual goal of union with God, who is spirit. The work of salvation, then, is to transcend material, mortal existence. It is about the elevation of spirit and the denigration of flesh, the transcendence of the divinely immaterial and immortal soul over the diabolically material and mortal body. The transhumanist project of disembodying and unearthing our minds, of transcending our Earth-born, Earth-bound biological bodies through radical extension, is a kind of high-tech post-Christian Gnosticism.

A mysticism, moreover, that illustrates Marx's view of religion as opiate, that is, as false consciousness that masks our perception of material and economic realities. Transhumanist visions of transcendence mask the true planetary costs of the technologies that they imagine will achieve such a vision. As Jussi Parikka and Kate Crawford remind us, technologies are not only extensions of the human; they are extensions of the earth, the geophysical world, and of life and labor.[20] Often represented as disembodied and immaterial, moving through digital networks and dwelling in clouds, the new and emerging technologies of what Crawford aptly describes as a massive super-system of "planetary computation" that passes today as artificial intelligence is built not only from mined data but also from mined earth, labor, and life, often backed by military force. It is driven by the ambition "to capture the planet in a computationally legible form . . . as a centralized God's-eye view of human movement, communication, and labor."[21] As such it is a continuation earlier capitalist modes of state and corporate extraction in the name of infinite growth.

GODS OF THE ANTHROPOCENE

We are the gods now. Or will soon be. Godlikeness has become, or will soon become, godhood. Other than that, the key tenets of the modern biblical dominion delusion remain largely intact in our time of technocratic optimism: distinct from and exceptional to all other creatures, we are the center of our universe, blessed with and responsible for dominion, destined for eternal fruitfulness. We are continuing to fulfill Bacon's call, which he believed to be from God but we now know to be intrinsic to us, to restore ourselves to Paradise. Only it will be a paradise of our own making.

Remember that the first calls to embrace our true divinity came in the early aftermath of the first half of the twentieth century, a time marked by so many epiphanies of our new techno-scientific potential for military and genocidal violence and destruction. These decades also mark the dawning of the Anthropocene, a new era in which anthropogenic influences on the planet's ecological and geological systems are more powerful than any nonhuman forces.

Gods can save, but they can also destroy. They can transcend, but they can also descend and incend, bringing the rest of creation down in flames with them.

Wouldn't it be something if, just as we begin to assume our divinity, we also bring about our own end, our own extinction? We are the gods now. Gods of the Anthropocene. Gods of our own undoing.

◆

4

GODS WITH ANUSES

"You are gods, children of the most high, all of you;
still, you shall die as humans . . ."

—Psalm 82:6–7[1]

O NCE WE BELIEVED we were like God, created in God's image, blessed and charged with godlike dominion over creation.
Then we believed we might as well *be* gods. After all, God himself
basically admitted we could be, which is why we were expelled from
Eden and thereby kept from the tree of eternal life. Maybe, we began
to think, we can do a better job. So the biblical charter of foundation
was expanded into a new narrative arc of salvation: from the earlier
naive belief in being created in the image of God to the realization
that we *are* the gods, and as such the authors of our own providence.

But biblical stories are slippery things. The more tightly you hold
them, the more likely they are to evade your grasp. They resist final,
conclusive interpretations. There is always within them another "yes,
but . . ." So it is with the story of the so-called fall and expulsion
from Eden.

The nineteenth-century Danish philosopher and theologian
Søren Kierkegaard raised a serious "yes, but" to the biblical interpretation of godlike human exceptionalism. This story, he argued, is not
about humankind's fall from grace through sin and rebellion. Rather,

it is about our fall into self-consciousness, through which we become aware of a fundamental problem with our aspirations to divinity: our mortality and inevitable death. Yes, we are as gods, able to expand our consciousness to transcend time and space, to contemplate the mysteries of nature and the origins of the universe. But we are at the same time destined to descend again, to fall back to the ground, to die and decompose mindlessly like any other animal, returning to the soil from which we came. For Kierkegaard, then, the Garden of Eden story is about the fundamental *paradox* of human existence, as inescapable as it is dreadful: that we are simultaneously god and worm, reaching for heaven but doomed to compost. It is the story of our fall into the inescapable knowledge of our own mortality.[2]

In his Pulitzer Prize–winning book *The Denial of Death*, the late psychologist Ernest Becker delved more deeply into the unbearable terror of this paradoxical existence and the ways we struggle, individually and collectively, to evade or repress it. His argument was as follows.

First, the natural world is a living nightmare of violence, of eating and being eaten. "What are we to make of a creation," Becker writes,

> in which the routine activity is for organisms to be tearing others apart with teeth of all types—biting, grinding flesh, plant stalks, bones between molars, pushing the pulp greedily down the gullet with delight, incorporating its essence into one's own organization, and then excreting with foul stench and gasses the residue . . . not to mention the daily dismemberment and slaughter in "natural" accidents of all types.[3]

Seen from this elevation, creation is a mind-boggling bloodbath of murder, death, consumption, and rot, of life entwined with death.

Second, like Kierkegaard, Becker believed that human consciousness makes us feel that we stand out from the rest of creation like gods. We think and act beyond our own narrow perceptions. We surmise about pasts and futures we are not part of, about scales of time and space beyond our bodily existence. The human "is a creator with a mind that soars out to speculate about atoms and infinity, who can place himself imaginatively at a point in space and contemplate bemusedly his own planet." Our remarkable dexterity, enabling us to expand beyond ourselves to contemplate everything from the microscopic to the galactic, imbues us with "the status of a small god in nature, as the Renaissance thinkers knew."[4]

> [The human] not only lives in this moment, but expands his inner self to yesterday, his curiosity to centuries ago, his fears to five billion years from now when the sun will cool, his hopes to an eternity from now. He lives not only on a tiny territory, nor even on an entire planet, but in a galaxy, in a universe, and in dimensions beyond visible universes.[5]

Yet, along with our godlike consciousness as symbolic selves comes another kind of awareness that the rest of creation does not possess: the terrible knowledge of our mortality, that we do not stay gods forever, that our ultimate destiny is to become food for worms.

> This is the paradox: he is out of nature and hopelessly in it; he is dual, up in the stars and yet housed in a heart-pumping, breath-gasping body that once belonged to a fish and still carries the gill-marks to prove it. His body is a material fleshy casing that is alien to him in many ways—the strangest and most repugnant way being that it aches and bleeds and will decay and die. Man is literally split in two: he has an awareness of his own splendid uniqueness in that he sticks out of nature with a towering majesty, and yet he goes back into the ground a few feet in order blindly and dumbly to rot and disappear forever. It is a terrifying dilemma to be in and to have to live with.[6]

This animal-doomed-to-rot side of our human existence is powerfully signified for us in the fact that we eat and shit. The "meaning of anality" is that, as far as nature is concerned, we are bodies like other bodies, entirely earthbound, part of the same cycle of life to death to decay to life as any other plant or animal.

> Nature's values are bodily values, human values are mental values, and though they take the loftiest flights they are built upon excrement, impossible without it, always brought back to it. . . . The anus and its incomprehensible, repulsive product represents not only physical determinism and boundness, but the fate as well of all that is physical: decay and death . . . to fashion the sublime miracle of the human face . . . to bring this out of nothing, out of the void, and make it shine in noonday; to take such a miracle and put miracles again within it, deep in the mystery of eyes that peer out—the eye that gave even the dry Darwin a chill: to do all this, and to combine it with an anus that shits! It is too much. Nature mocks us, and poets live in torture.[7]

The paradox of the human condition is that we are gods who shit, or, as Becker famously put it, "gods with anuses."[8]

IMMORTALITY PROJECTS

Becker believed that if humankind were to face this reality directly, we would collectively go insane. The world would literally catch fire and it'd be over for us. The reality of our paradoxical condition is simply unbearable for human society as a whole. And so what drives us above all else, individually and collectively, is the deep and abiding need to suppress that reality, to deny our wormly mortality and to elevate our exceptional godlikeness.

Which brings us to the third point in Becker's argument. In response to the unbearable reality of the paradoxical human condition, we create various "immortality vehicles" or "hero systems" as means of transcending death and achieving a sense of enduring "cosmic specialness." We fight and die in battle for the sake of our values, our folk, our land, our country, and our God. We send our own children and grandchildren to the front lines to do the same. If and when they are wounded or die, we consecrate the tragedy by calling it a sacrifice (from the Latin *sacri-facere,* to "make sacred"). Likewise when we submit to austerity measures or cuts in pay for the sake of the economy, whether during wartime, pandemic-induced depression, or some other national emergency.

Or we attach our deep, mostly sublimated desire for cosmic specialness to an object of romantic love. The loved one is lifted up, indeed beatified as the idealization of divinity, for whom I eagerly devote my very life. I am saved not through some abstract god but by this incarnation of true love. As the biblical Song of Songs puts it, "Love is as strong as death and passion is as fierce as the grave" (8:6). Through the romantic solution to the human condition, spirituality becomes this-worldly. Death is transcended by losing oneself in the love of another.

Or we devote all our heart, mind, and strength to the heroic pursuit of creative genius. The artist transcends mortality by transcending common humanity through the godlike creation of an immortal work of art, which becomes a monument to their unique individual brilliance. The artist stands apart from the masses with their common ways of seeing the world. The artist's work is a form of "personal immortality," creating a personal "beyond" that is not shared with others.[9] The artist's immortality vehicle is a one-seater, a kind of individual, private religion of their own making.

Or we pursue immortality by devoting our lives to lasting fortunes in our names. Or promoting democracy or global capitalism or communism. Or realizing true artificial intelligence. They are all immortality vehicles, driven by the need to transcend the finite time and space of this mortal coil.

That in itself would be plenty to try to take in. But there's another, more disturbing paradox that follows: *all such heroic immortality projects, aimed at overcoming mortal suffering and death, ultimately bring about even greater suffering and death.* Contrary to common belief,

Becker insisted, violence and war are not brought on by giving in to our "lower" animal natures; rather, they are brought on by our drive to transcend that nature, to deny and finally overcome our mortal animality. As Sam Keen comments, "Our desire for the best is the cause of the worst. We want to clean up the world, make it perfect, keep it safe for democracy or communism, purify it of the enemies of god, eliminate evil, establish an alabaster city undimmed by human tears, or a thousand year Reich."[10] The cost is always more violence, more suffering, more death.

IT'S ALL RELIGION

Religious traditions have often been powerful cultural vehicles for our collective denial of creaturely mortality, shared systems of what Freud described as wish fulfillment, giving expression to that which we deeply, indeed mostly subconsciously, wish were true.

Becker saw Christianity as an especially effective immortality vehicle: Like the incarnate Christ, who was fully human and fully God, the Christian follower believes they come from God into the world and will eventually return to God.[11] They live out their life in devotion and obedience to God. Upon death, they shed this mortal coil to meet God. Facing judgment, they are justified by faith and rewarded with eternal life, basking in the heavenly light of divine grace forever. The former life in this vale of tears no longer matters, is but a distant fleeting memory. Christianity, in this view, is able to be an essentially universal hero system. Rich or poor, slave or free, weak or mighty, anyone can become the death-transcending hero. Indeed, this system embraces the very mortal creatureliness that we desperately seek to deny and makes it the vehicle for its own transcendence, a necessary passageway through which we achieve immortality.

That religions per se often function as immortality projects is no great revelation. But Becker's point was far more radical: *any and every cultural system* is likewise *essentially religious*, insofar as it functions to deny mortality and death by transcending it. This is because "civ-ilized" society, no matter how ostensibly secular or anti-religious, "is a hopeful belief and protest that science, money and goods make man count for more than any other animal. In this sense everything that man does is religious and heroic."[12] Whether built on communism or capitalism, consumerism or asceticism, Christianity or Islam, domin-ionism or transhumanism, such systems are living myths of human exceptionalism, illusory means for denying the ultimate reality of hu-man creatureliness. It's all religion.

DENIAL OF DEATH AS A SPECIES

The diagnosis: beneath all our cultural systems, whether ostensibly religious, nonreligious, or anti-religious, is the fundamentally reli-gious drive to solve the problem of the human condition, which is our paradoxical godlike animality and animal godlikeness, our will to immortality and transcendence housed in a body that dies and rots.

Although Becker focused clearly and incisively on the social psy-chology of our denial of death as individuals, it is easy to see how that denial is inextricably bound up with our denial of death as a species. Indeed, our individual denial of mortality, and all the immortality delusions it drives, requires the same denial on the species level. Our denial of death as a species is our individual denial of death writ large, precisely because human finitude threatens to undermine any and all of our immortality projects with inevitable, ultimate oblivion in the form of extinction.

Nothing we can do or be is monumental enough to endure long past our extinction—with the modest exception, perhaps, of the sig-nature geological layer of concrete, plastic, carbon, and fallout that we will leave behind. Like our bodies, the grandest works of human civilizations will decay and return to the ground to feed new forms of life. No matter how high and mighty, they will eventually be over-taken by wildernesses of forest and desert and sea, which swallows the monuments under green and gray, slowly digesting them back to earth.[13] The truth of this reality is all around us, from cracks in city walls and sidewalks where little green sprouts are taking hold, to *tells* (Arabic for hills or mounds) formed by layer upon layer of ruined civilizations, sometimes going back as far as the Neolithic era more than twelve thousand years ago.

Are we not collectively repressing our mortality as a species ever more intensely as it becomes more imminent? In these our twilight years, our immortality vehicles are running on jet fuel. Our **wonder** and **awe** at our own accomplishments is in bold denial of the growing insecurity that drives them.

And is not this desperate denial of our finitude leading paradoxically to greater violence and suffering in the world, for much of the human population as well as for other forms of earthly life? Our insistence on unsustainable practices, driven by the twin pillars of capitalist faith, extraction and infinite growth, generate untold harm against the ecologies that we exploit in order to maintain that faith. No need to remake the case or provide more examples of how this works. It's a simple logic: the faith in infinite growth that drives the economy is delusional and can only be maintained by exploiting the lives and livelihoods of others. It is an immortality project of infinite growth fueled by extraction.

Our denial of death as a species is fundamentally unsustainable. The more forcefully we assert our godlike human exceptionalism against the inescapable realities of earthly finitude, the more forcefully the latter comes back upon us. Our finally unexceptional, nonexempt status as a species is inescapable. All our immortality vehicles will break down and rust away. The ground from which we came will have the last word, claiming them and us as its own.

Once we believed we were like God. Now some say we *are* the gods. Perhaps, but gods with anuses. God worms. Manic gods on the verge of insanity, sciencing the shit out of the bed we have made for ourselves.

RELIGION AS MORTALITY PROJECT

All immortality vehicles are religious, driven by the desire to escape the fundamental, inescapable paradox of the human condition, our mud-godness. Whether by dominion or transcendence or both, whether by special blessing from God or by becoming gods, they are wish-fulfillment projects, means of denying, overcoming, and transcending mortality and death, as individuals and as a species.

If all immortality vehicles are religious, is all religion about building and fueling immortality vehicles? Is that all religion has to offer? Becker, who died of colon cancer at the age of forty-nine, shortly after finishing *The Denial of Death*, did not think so.[14] In the last pages of his book, he envisioned a "fusion" of scientific and religious dispositions that might be able to hold together, on the one hand, the *mystery* of lived experience and, on the other, the *reality* of its inevitable end in death. Such a disposition, simultaneously religious and scientific, would allow us to remain open and available to wonder and awe in the face of a reality that will ultimately overtake and transcend us—as Becker put it, to "wait in a condition of openness toward miracle and mystery, in the lived truth of creation." By "the lived truth of creation," he meant precisely the world as we experience it when we are not in denial of our humble place within it. It is the world "as it would appear to creatures who assessed their true puniness in the face of the overwhelmingness and majesty of the universe."[15] To be alive in this way demands that we open ourselves not only to love and wonder but also to pain, fear, and grief. Anything more self-aggrandizing, anything more heroic, would be a retreat back into self-deception and denial.

Can religion also be a resource for *mortality projects*? Can religion open us to both the awesome wonder and the unexceptional reality of the lived truth of creation? Can religion put us in closer touch with our own finitude, not only as individuals but also as a species? Can it help us come to terms with our mortal earthiness in all its terrible beauty? These are the questions that will occupy us from here forward.

◆

5

PALLIATIVE HOPE

O NCE WE BELIEVED we were like God. Now we believe we are the gods. Gods with anuses. Mud-gods.

Where does this leave us? What ways forward are available to us? Are we left only to hope for some sort of provisional pretense of sanity, knowing that it's only possible by continuing to live in denial? Just try to keep sleeping, keep dreaming, keep building and driving our immortality vehicles, as if they will save us?

Or do we give up and party like there's no tomorrow? Say to hell with everyone and everything else, withdraw all our savings, both real and proverbial, and go out in a prodigal blaze of glory? Everyone for themselves. Every nation for itself. Whether we're talking about policies with global implications or everyday activities like grocery shopping and recycling, it's tempting to take this to-hell-with-it-all turn. As my friend recently lamented, "I could buy only shampoo bars in cardboard boxes for my whole family, but there will still be too much plastic in the ocean, so fuck it. Which is where I go sometimes." What's the point in trying if we're done for anyway?

Continue dreaming or give in to nihilism—are these the only alternatives? One kind of denial or the other? In the Anthropocene, are these our only real options? Is this, as Nick Mulvey asks in his song "In the Anthropocene," all our freedom has come to mean? I hope not.

A PARABLE OF THE HUMAN SITUATION

Lars von Trier's movie *Melancholia* (2011) is the story of two sisters in the days before a rogue planet named Melancholia crashes into Earth and smashes it to pieces. Justine (played by Kirsten Dunst) is chronically depressed, while her sister Claire (played by Charlotte Gainsbourg) is her proverbial opposite—together, responsible, and prosperous. The story begins as Melancholia has just passed close by, barely missing Earth. Soon, however, it becomes clear that the planet is circling back. In a matter of days, Melancholia and Earth will collide, destroying all life.

Claire's husband (played by Kiefer Sutherland), an optimist who up to this point had flatly dismissed all the doomsday predictions, commits suicide by overdosing on Claire's pills, leaving her, their young son, and her sister Justine alone to face the end. As the last days unfold and reality sinks in, the two sisters' states of mind seem to reverse: Claire is paralyzed by depression and anxiety, while Justine gains a new sense of clear-minded peace and composure. In a small yet powerful final act of grace, Justine builds a teepee-shaped open frame from sticks on a small grassy knoll for Claire, Claire's son, and herself. Like a minister hosting a final ritual, she embraces her two companions and escorts them into the makeshift sacred space. They sit silently together in a small circle, holding hands, while Melancholia grows ever larger on the horizon. As the end draws near, the camera pulls back, showing their silhouettes in the little teepee frame against the cratered backdrop of the approaching planet, which fills the sky. In the final seconds, as Richard Wagner's prelude to the opera *Tristan and Isolde* crescendos, Claire panics, letting go of their hands, rocking frantically while sobbing. Her son and Justine remain calm, still holding hands. Roaring white heat fills the screen, and then everything goes dark.

Sometimes described as a psychological disaster movie, *Melancholia* is really a parable of the human situation. Lars von Trier developed the idea for it while suffering from debilitating depression. He wanted to explore the different ways we might change if we were to know with certainty that the end—not just our own individual ends but our end as a species—were at hand. What if it really is too late? What if our end is imminent, whether in eight days, eighty days, eighty years, or maybe even eight hundred years? Might we be surprised by ourselves and others? Could it bring clarity and peace of mind for some who have lived lives of anxiety or depression? On the other hand, could it bring disorientation and panic for some who have lived lives of prosperity and security? What resources, spiritual and otherwise, that have sustained us in relative denial of humankind's fragility and impermanence might prove useless on this new horizon? What others might prove indispensable? Where and how would we find hope that does not need to presume that humankind will go on forever?

DESIGN CUES

I've come to believe that our way forward has to be something of a palliative approach to the human future.

In healthcare, palliative medicine for an individual begins by affirming the inevitability of death as a normal part of life and prioritizes quality of life over quantity or duration of life. Thus it aims to alleviate unnecessary suffering, to learn to live with necessary suffering, to avoid isolation, and to find community, often integrating psychological and spiritual dimensions into the caregiving process. As Atul Gawande puts it, a palliative approach is not simply a matter of asking, "What do you want when you are dying?" Rather, it invites us to ask, "If time becomes short, what is most important to you?"[1]

Palliative hope is far from defeatist. It is not about giving up. It is not simply about how to die. It is about how to live when you know that death is inevitable, whether in the coming days, weeks, or even years. It is about breaking through the denial of death, accepting that death is part of life. It is holistic, focusing not only on physical survival but also on psychological, social, and spiritual well-being in the context of one's community. Far from fatalistic or gloomy, such an approach is deeply, realistically hopeful, driven by faith in the possibility of a meaningful, terminal future.

What can we learn about how to approach species mortality from the insights and practices of individual palliative care? What might a palliative approach to the human future look like? B. J. Miller, a palliative care physician and former director of the Zen Hospice Project, offers three "design cues" for individual palliative care that I find suggestive in beginning to explore this question.[2]

The first design cue is "teasing unnecessary suffering out of the system." In palliative healthcare, this often means deciding against risky or expensive procedures that might add some longevity at the expense of comfort and quality of life. A palliative approach to the human future might begin to ask, How much suffering do we generate, or allow to be generated, in the service of our delusions of godlike immortality—delusions that only a select few have the privilege of believing in anyway? How much unnecessary suffering is required by this system of denial of death as a species? How much harm to other beings, animate and inanimate, and to other humans—indeed to whole cultures and continents—do we cause through the ever-accelerating practices of exploitation and extraction that feed our pursuit of immortality through infinite growth?

Second is the importance of "tending to dignity by way of the senses, by way of the body." This is the realm of *aesthetics*. Aesthetics (from the Greek *aesthesis*, "sensation") is not just about the appreciation of beauty; it is about embodied, sensory experience. "As long as we have our senses, even just one," Miller says, "we have at least the possibility of accessing what makes us feel human, connected."

As we have seen, the denial of death is often expressed through the denial of the body. This denial is most explicit in the transhumanist movement, which aspires to transcend biology and therefore mortality. And yet, while transhumanists may be among the most extreme examples, they are not the only ones whose cultural systems belie a desire to transcend bodily existence—to *anesthetize* ourselves to the human condition. Transhumanism is simply the latest flagship for our modern Western denial of humankind's embeddedness in the natural world. Consumerism is our mass culture version of transhumanism. We anesthetize ourselves to our mortality and finitude through our obsessive, insatiable consumption of things that promise to renew and recreate us, from "anti-aging" products promising younger, tighter skin and stronger bodies, to luxury brands that promise to lift us out of and over the unwashed masses, poor souls. The pursuit of wealth, which we demonstrate to ourselves and others through the goods and services we consume, is a form of death denial—"terror management," as psychologists put it.[3] Life in abundance in pursuit of life everlasting. This, paradoxically, is a denial of what Miller calls "dignity by way of the senses." It is the numbing antithesis of being mindfully embodied in the world, which subjects us to the aliveness of hunger and cold as well as of good food and drink, warm blankets, and warm bodies.

Which brings us to the third design cue, beneficence: to "set our sights on well-being" rather than on disease, so that "caring becomes a creative, generative, even playful act." Since we cannot "solve for death," transhumanists notwithstanding, we should focus on beneficence, that is, the creative furtherance of well-being, making life better and fuller. We do this not despite our human finitude, individual and collective, but in the mindful presence of it.

To tease out unnecessary suffering. To tend to dignity by way of the body, the senses. To pursue beneficence, the creative furtherance of well-being in the face of the inevitable. Are these design cues for individual palliative care not translatable to a palliative approach to the human future? First, we must sort out necessary versus unnecessary suffering (human and nonhuman) in our local, national, and global systems, and work to alleviate that which is unnecessary, especially when such unnecessary suffering is caused by exploitative and extractive actions and policies championed by the most powerful among us in the pursuit of unnecessary and excessive comfort. Second, we must resist our modern inclination to deny our mortality and finitude, as individuals and as a species, by denying our biological embodiment and ecological interdependence. Third, we must reorient ourselves, turning from our delusional immortality vehicles and setting our sights on beneficence, that is, designing and creating for well-being in the face of finitude.

As with individual palliative care, part of a palliative approach to the human future involves practical, policy-oriented conversations on local, national, and global levels. I most certainly am not an expert on this front. But I think a good place to begin such conversations is to ask a palliative-minded question: As time becomes short, what really matters for our communities and our world?

We might not need to drill for oil in the Arctic National Wildlife Refuge. But we might want to restore the habitat of the Alaskan wood bison, which have lived interdependently with the Athabascan people for more than ten thousand years. Too little, too late, to be sure. Still, there is value in confessing, repenting, and seeking justice, perhaps especially as time becomes short.

We won't get to ride into and beyond the sunset to a new planetary home in another solar system, leaving Mother Nature behind, as Neil Young envisioned in his haunting lament "After the Gold Rush." Nor will there be time to wait for the scientists to open a door onto some other viable way forward, as Modest Mouse sardonically imagined in "Lampshades on Fire." But we might get better at practicing neighborliness.

We might not make America great again, if it ever was. But we might commit what time and resources we have left to reparations for the slavery of Black people and the displacement and genocide of Native American peoples.

We might not biomedically solve for death for the elite few who could afford it. But we might discover and implement new ways to dramatically improve the quality of life for people in poverty around the world.

Closer to home for me, what if churches and other religious communities were to take seriously our finite human future? In many ways, churches are immortality projects par excellence. Too often their priestly and lay leaders are focused almost exclusively on how to continue as though forever: how to maintain their land and buildings, how to grow their endowments, how to add more parking spots. This is as true for big, growing congregations as it is for those whose member rolls have dwindled to a tiny remnant of old faithfuls. They might not even like each other! But they are united in their addiction to perpetuity. Whether growing or shrinking, what if churches were to shift their perspective, to act as if time is short, which it is, not only for them but for all of us? How might it change their priorities? What might they do differently with their property and other resources? With their energy? What would Jesus do?

One thing I am certain of is that any such shared priorities and policies cannot be motivated or justified by the delusional goals of infinite economic growth and the infinite extension of human life. However ecofriendly such political visions claim to be, they are immortality projects, built on a foundation of faith in human exceptionalism, fueled by denial. The now familiar wartime rhetoric of "defeating" or "beating" climate change while growing the economy with new "green jobs" should be telling here.

Beyond policies and programs, we also need to pursue new ways of seeing ourselves and our world. We need new stories, ones that are not, as Naomi Klein aptly put it, "ways of looking away," however well-intentioned.[4] We need to fund our imaginations with alternative ways of seeing and being in the world that can help us break through the denial, allow us to grieve what has been lost and will be lost, and help us find hope even as time becomes short.

Part of this work is about creative *remaking*, that is, taking received traditions and stories that no longer quite hold, no longer quite make sense, and using them, or pieces of them, to create new imaginative spaces in which to re-vision our situation and live meaningfully into it.[5] This is where I hope to have something to contribute.

CULTIVATING EARTH CREATURELINESS

With this interest in mind, I want to return to the religious traditions from which the big story of dominion and human exceptionalism was extracted in order to draw out a very different biblical understanding of what it means to be human, one that is alive to what Becker called "the lived truth of creation." I call it earth creatureliness. As we will see, this religious worldview unfolds in a series of interrelationships and interdependencies that interrogate the modern Western theology of dominionism even as they resonate with other indigenous religious traditions.

First, earth creatureliness affirms the inseparability of human and nonhuman beings, animate and inanimate. This awareness is expressed through a biblical poetics of intersubjectivity that conceives of nonhuman beings—from animals, to trees, to rivers and seas, to earth and land, to light and darkness—as subjects who are in relationship with humans and with the divine. This tradition imagines God interacting not only with humans but also with nonhuman creatures and things. It envisions animate and inanimate beings interacting with one another, with humans, and with God. Trees clap their hands and skip like deer. Mountains shout. The sea boasts. The land rests, and grieves, and might at any moment spit us humans out if we don't start behaving. Together these voices fund the imagination with visions of a wild world ecology of intersubjective creation.[6]

Second, earth creatureliness understands the interconnectedness of life and death. Life and death are intertwined. Life comes from death, depends on death, even feeds on it. The soil from which the human is formed is the soil to which it returns. The earth's topsoil is a planetary compost fertilized by every plant and animal that has ever lived. New life comes from it and returns to it. Biblical tradition understands this reality as the lived truth of creation, which is always re-creation, new life from death.

Third, earth creatureliness recognizes the inseparability of environmental justice and social justice. Social justice and human well-being are inextricably bound up with ecological and cosmological well-being. Human thriving, ecological thriving, and cosmic thriving resonate with and reflect one another. Likewise, human injustice can undo the entire ecological and cosmological integrity of creation. As we will see with the biblical prophets, social injustice, especially the systemic oppression of poor and marginalized persons by the ruling elite, can bring the whole world down with it. The sun goes dark, the chaos waters rise, and the land mourns in response to unjust human practices of exploitation and extraction.

Fourth and finally, earth creatureliness understands the interconnectedness of newness and impermanence. The potential emergence of wonderful, surprising new things is bound up with the reality of fleetingness. Biblical metaphors for transience and impermanence speak not only to the reality of finitude and mortality but also to renewal and newness. There is a grasslikeness to everything we wish would last forever. It can burn or dry up or be washed away. Our earth-creaturely grasslikeness reminds us of our fragile impermanence. At the same time, it can also awaken us to ever-present possibilities of newness. Isaiah imagines God pouring water on a thirsty land and its inhabitants suddenly springing up, grasslike. Grasslikeness is impermanence, and grasslikeness is the necessary condition for the arrival of astonishing new things.

For those of us who identify with the religious traditions of Judaism or Christianity, for whom these texts are core scriptures, this biblical earth creatureliness can be a powerful means of beginning to reorient ourselves away from human exceptionalism and toward theologies and practices of ecological interdependence.

For those who do not necessarily relate to these traditions as scripture, I still believe they can be resources for creating new imaginative spaces in which to reconceive ourselves in ways that are both realistic and hopeful. Indeed, they join a chorus of other religious voices, ancient and contemporary, that can inform what Bron Taylor calls "dark green religion," which he describes as a kind of spirituality that gives expression to and flows from "a deep sense of belonging to and connectedness in nature, while perceiving the earth and its living systems to be sacred and interconnected."[7]

I'm not advocating for the recovery and cultivation of earth creatureliness because I think it will necessarily save us from our ecological crisis. I don't believe that we will sufficiently decelerate, let alone reverse, the great anthropogenic acceleration in which we find ourselves, though I'd be very happy to discover otherwise. Whether or not that is possible, I do believe that cultivating this kind of earth creatureliness as a way of being in the world can help us break through our ideology of human exceptionalism, our denial of human finitude, and our otherwise inevitable panic and despair with reality, grief, and hope.

◆

6

BACK TO THE BEGINNINGS

B EFORE WE can open up new imaginative spaces in which to
discover alternatives to our delusions of godlike dominion and
human exceptionalism, we should first revisit the biblical stories that
have, for so long now, served those delusions. We need to go back and
try to break up some of that hard-packed, heavily trodden biblical
ground to see if something else might grow there.

GENESISES

Ask almost anyone and they'll tell you that there is only one biblical
account of creation. Whether or not they've ever read it, they'll also
agree that it says that humans were created uniquely in the image of
God and commanded to subdue and have dominion over the rest of
creation. They might believe in and embrace this account, or they
might reject it, blaming it for global capitalism, climate crisis, and
many other related woes brought on by Christianity. Still, love it or
hate it, most agree that this is the one and only biblical version of
creation.

The fact is that there are several very different, even contradictory ways of imagining creation in the Bible. We find them not only
at the beginning of the book of Genesis but also in Psalms, Proverbs,

and the book of Job. They don't all add up to a single account of creation. They don't even agree in basic outline and general details.[1]

Even when we narrow our focus to the opening few chapters of Genesis, the first "book" in both Jewish and Christian scriptures, what we find is not one creation story but two very different ones. In the first (Genesis 1:1–2:4a), humans are created in the image of God, male and female, on the sixth and final day, after God has created everything else, including plants and animals.[2] In the second (Genesis 2:4b–3:24), by contrast, a single human is created first, even before plants begin to grow. God then forms animals as potential companions for the human. When that doesn't work, God divides the human into two, one female and one male, and they become companions for one another.

The two stories also have very different literary styles and use different Hebrew names for the divine creator. The first uses 'elohim, which is both a proper name, "God," and a plural noun, "gods." The second, by contrast uses yhwh 'elohim, which is typically translated into English as "LORD God," using "LORD" in small capitals instead of "Yahweh" out of respect for Jewish prohibitions against saying the sacred proper name out loud.

In fact, these two creation myths began as unrelated stories, separated by centuries, before they were edited together into the beginning of Genesis. Most scholars agree that the second story is centuries older than the first, likely originating in the context of highland farming culture to the west of the Jordan River. Scholars debate the historical origins of the first story in its final form, which could date as late as the Babylonian exile, after the fall of the southern kingdom of Judah (587 BCE).

Why would these two very different stories of beginnings, coming from two very different times and places, be set back-to-back in the first two chapters of Genesis, with no apparent effort to sync them up? Even a quick search-and-replace of "'elohim" for "yhwh 'elohim" or vice versa would have done wonders to smooth the transition from one to the next. Were the many ancient scribes and redactors of these texts just so stupid, so inattentive to details that they didn't notice the glaring discrepancies? It's modern arrogance to think so.[3]

One answer could be that, by the time the Hebrew scriptures were taking form, both stories were already so familiar and treasured on their own terms, with all their major differences, that no one dared alter them significantly. They were sacrosanct against line editing and proofreading. That may well have been so.

But a more obvious reason is that the value of these stories had little to do with consistency, let alone with anything like a uniform scientific explanation of origins. When people today argue for biblical creation against Darwinian evolutionary theory, they are not defending the Bible; they are misunderstanding it. These stories are not scientific accounts of cosmic or human beginnings. Rather, they are creative, mythopoetic renderings of the world. Their value lies not in their power to explain origins but in their capacity to fund poetic imagination, to see and experience the world in new ways. As if to say, "Here's a story. Now here's another one." In these opening chapters of Genesis, the Bible we have inherited does not seem to have a problem with that.

I've learned the hard way that many people today *do* have a problem with that. Several years ago I was invited to write a short piece for a popular online men's lifestyle magazine, "Five Things You Didn't Know About the Bible." Although this topic seemed pretty far afield of the magazine's main core subjects, namely sex, dating, and manscaping, I decided to give it a shot.

The first of my five things was that there are multiple accounts of creation in the Bible. Given my own background in conservative evangelical Christian culture, I expected some people to disagree, but I did not anticipate the flood of enraged responses, especially in a magazine that didn't strike me as remotely conservative, let alone Christian. Once I got over being called a "gay moron" and "fatass nerd editor sitting in his basement," I could see that my critics assumed that I was some kind of Bible-bashing atheist whose goal was to "make the Bible look stupid, irrelevant, and full of holes" as if it's "a load of bullshit." There was zero interest in engaging with the logic of my argument, let alone the biblical texts that I used to support it. As one exclaimed, "the OP [original poster, me] needs to actually check his facts. You would think one might actually read the books objectively before commenting on them. Seriously??? Differences in Gen 1&2??? Are you nuts!!!" Several made clear that my attack on the Bible was also an attack on its presumed author, God, and therefore on faith in general. Never mind that I'm actually Christian, that I regularly teach about the Bible in confirmation classes and Sunday school, and that I've dedicated half my life to studying and teaching biblical literature as a college professor. As they saw it, I was putting the Bible on trial, calling out its contradictions and thereby undermining its credibility. For them, as for many others, the Bible stands or falls, triumphs or fails, on the question of whether or not it contradicts itself.

But you can't fail at something you're not trying to do. To ask whether the Bible fails to give consistent answers or to be of one voice with itself presumes that it was built to do so. That's a false presumption, rooted no doubt in thinking of it as the book that God wrote. The Bible is constantly interpreting, interrogating, and disagreeing with itself.

So it is when it comes to the two very different, literally contradictory creation stories in Genesis. We need to go back and look at each more closely, expecting them to contradict, expecting them to offer very different poetic conceptions of creation and what it means to be human in the world.

We also need to reflect more critically on how these two stories relate to our bankrupt big story of godlike dominion and human exceptionalism. In so doing, we will see that the dominionist interpretive tradition largely misreads the first story, the one in which humans are created in God's image and commanded to subdue and have dominion. When we read it more closely, the dominionist reading is a stretch, to say the least. We will also see how the second story, when it is allowed to stand on its own rather than as a continuation of the first, funds our imaginations with a poetics of earth creatureliness that radically undermines any delusions of dominion or human exceptionalism. Human spirituality in this story is both intimately related to the divine and grounded in the earth from which life emerges and to which it returns.

DOMINION DOWNGRADE

Dominion theology—the idea that humans are created uniquely like God and given godlike rule over the rest of creation—is built on a very tiny bit of Bible, namely, a couple of verses in the first creation story in Genesis (1:1–2:4a) and a couple more verses in one of the Psalms (8:5–6).[4] Biblically inspired claims to exceptional godlike dominion ultimately come down to these few verses, which have gotten huge traction, especially in the modern West, in driving our immortality vehicles. They are the biblical basis of our grand narrative of godlike dominion and human exceptionalism. They are therefore most in need of rereading in context. To do so, we will need to wade a little ways into some somewhat academic thickets related to Hebrew words and questions of translation.[5]

The familiar Christian synopsis of the first creation story in Genesis goes something like this:

> God, who is all-powerful, all-knowing, and all-good, created the world in all its complexity from nothing (*ex nihilo*). That world, like its creator, is one of meaningful order and symmetry. Yet God does not inhabit this creation. Spirit and matter are entirely separate. God, who is eternal spirit, is categorically different from and infinitely superior to the material world.
>
> The process of creation moved from the general and cosmic to the particular, unfolding over the course of six days: separating light from dark and day from night; separating the waters above (the heavens) from the waters below; separating the waters below from the dry land, which then brings forth vegetation of all kinds;

establishing the sun to govern the day and the moon and stars to govern the night; bringing forth all creatures of the sea and birds of the sky; creating all the land animals and, finally, creating humankind in God's own image.

That humankind was created in the image of God means that it is set apart from the rest of creation, blessed and commanded to rule over it like a god. "Be fruitful and multiply. Fill the earth and subdue it. Have dominion over the fish of the sea, and over the birds of the heavens, and over every living thing that creeps on the earth."

Indeed, humankind is the *reason* for creation, whose purpose is to be used and enjoyed by it. It is the stage on which humankind is to fulfill its divine calling to godlike dominion.

That's it in a nutshell, the biblical-theological foundation of human exceptionalism and godlike dominion over the rest of creation.

We should remember, moreover, that contemporary *secular* human exceptionalism is entirely compatible and congruent with this biblical theological version. The main reason for God in this story, after all, is to guarantee our godlikeness and dominion. In the wake of God, as we have seen, it is no great leap to assume the role for ourselves.

Now let's take a closer look at the biblical text from which this grand arc purportedly derives to see how it holds up.

First, what kind of creator is this God, and what kind of creative process is at work here? The dominionist interpretation imagines that this God is all-powerful and sovereign, and that he creates the world from nothing. This view, which goes back at least to the early Christian theologian and bishop Augustine of Hippo (d. 430 CE), is based on Latin and Greek translations of the Hebrew text.[6] In those translations, the sense is that God first creates the heavens and the earth from nothing, and that the earth, which God created from nothing, was initially formless and void. Then God proceeds to develop the earth into habitable formfulness, separating water from land, populating it with plants and animals, and so on. God, transcending time and space, acts as first cause, unmoved mover, creating the heavens and earth out of nothing and then proceeding to arrange them into cosmic order.

The Hebrew text, however, conjures a very different image, not of creation from nothing but emergence from chaos. How could it be so different from the Greek and Latin translations? It comes down to the very first Hebrew word in the story, *bere'šit* ("bᵉ-ray-sheet"), and how we read its very first letter, the *bet* ("b" sound), in relation to the rest of the word, *re'šit*. This word can be taken either as a noun, "beginning," or as a verb, "began." If you read it as a noun, as the Greek and Latin translations did, then you take the *bet* as a preposition, "in," and you get a simple declarative sentence familiar from the King James Version translation: "In the beginning God created the heaven and the earth." Full stop. What follows, "And the earth was without form, and void," then describes the unformed, chaotic (*tohu vabohu*) earth that God just created from nothing. Taken this way, then, we imagine an absolute beginning, with God creating heaven and earth from nothing. Which is how the Greek and Latin translations took it.

But if you read this first word as a verb, as most Hebrew biblical scholars argue you should, then the *bet* modifies that verb, and you get something like "when began." That leads to a translation something like, "When God began creating the heavens and the earth, the earth," which was already there when God began creating, "was formless void." Taken this way, we have a story that begins not at some absolute metaphysical beginning, with nothing, but in the midst of things, with God creating, or rather giving shape and form to, things that are already there in some sort of primordial formlessness. This offers an image of God as a co-creative participant with the material universe, interacting with each element of creation as it emerges and integrates within a larger ecosystem. This is not creation from nothing but emergence from chaos, with a creator God who is in relationship both with the material world and with the primordial deep from which it surfaces. God and matter are not categorically separate. On the contrary, they are intimately connected.

Second, how are we to understand the value of the nonhuman in relation to the human in this story? Is it, as the dominionist interpretation argues, a matter of use value? Are animals and the rest of creation there for humankind to use, a bounteous gift of "natural resources"? The fact that, after each stage of creation, God declares that it is all "good," in and of itself, without reference to humans, already suggests otherwise. Not once does God say, "The humans are going to love this! I can't wait to see what they do with it."

Indeed, God also blesses other living creatures before humankind is even created. Concerning the sea creatures and birds, God blessed them, saying, "Be fruitful and multiply and fill the waters in the seas, and birds will multiply in the earth" (1:22). Later, after God creates humans, God addresses all human *and* nonhuman animals together:

> God said, "See, I have given you every plant yielding seed that is upon the face of all the earth, and every tree with seed in its fruit; you shall have them for food. And to every beast of the earth, and to every bird of the air, and to everything that creeps on the earth, everything that has the breath of life, I have given every green plant for food." And it was so. (1:29–30; Revised Standard Version)

Notice: Not only are other animals blessed and commanded to thrive independent of humans; humans and animals alike are told by God to eat plants, not other animals. This is a strictly vegetarian vision of world ecology. No animals were harmed in the making of this creation story.

Which brings us to the dominion verse itself, which God addresses exclusively to the newly formed humans. Here it is in the familiar King James Version translation: "Be fruitful and multiply. Fill the earth and subdue it. Have dominion over the fish of the sea, and over the fowl of the air, and over every living thing that moveth upon the earth" (1:28). Let's take it apart.

Note that three of the five things humans are told to do—"be fruitful," "multiply," and "fill the earth"—were also commanded of the fish and birds earlier, before God created humans (1:22). These are not exceptional, exclusively human charges, but are what all living beings should do. Life is about bursting forth, growing, and filling. You could even argue that these are not really commandments at all but simply descriptions of what animal life naturally does. As in, "you do you."

The last two imperatives, however, are for humans only: "subdue" and "have dominion" or "rule" over other animals. What do these commands mean? The first, "subdue," from *kavaš*, essentially means what its Yiddishism suggests: to "put the kibosh" on something. To *kavaš* is to stamp down, to quash. Unfortunately, there is no kinder, gentler, more eco-friendly way to put it. "Subdue" is a pretty good translation. The second command, "have dominion" or "rule," from *radah*, is a little more complicated. As David M. Carr and others argue, this particular word (as distinct from *mašal*, which is also often translated as "rule") suggests an agonistic relationship with those ruled, who could otherwise threaten the ones ruling.[7] Here, then, between the lines and in context, both *kavaš* and *radah* suggest an attunement to the potentially dangerous and unpredictable wildness of other animals, a wildness that people who live in closer proximity to them know well.

How, then, should we imagine this subduing and ruling? For one thing, it is not about subduing or ruling over nonanimal parts of the environment. It does not command control over, let alone extraction of, "natural resources" like water, trees, and land, nor of the labor of other humans. It's about godlike human rule, or rather attempted rule, over other animals.

Nor can it mean killing and eating animals for food. God gives humans *and* other animals plants for food. After the flood, God will tell the human survivors to eat not only plants but also all other animals, who will live in fear of them (Genesis 9:1–3). But that's later. Whatever subduing and dominating of the other animals is being imagined in this story, it does not involve ranching or butchering, let alone anything like today's meat industry.

Perhaps it simply means fighting back, forcefully stopping an animal when it attacks a human.[8] Or maybe it means forcefully claiming human superiority and control over them within the larger ecology in which humans and animals of all kinds sometimes compete for survival. Or it could simply mean recognizing human superiority and dominance over other animals thanks to things like language, self-consciousness, use of tools, and opposable thumbs. This would be consistent with Carr's convincing case for translating God's creation of humans "as" rather than "in" God's image, "so that" they may subdue and rule over the animals in a role that is similar to that of divine rulership.[9]

A LITTLE LESS THAN GOD?

However we understand this command for humans to have dominion over other animals, we must also understand that the ancient context in which this story was first shared and told would have made any image of substantial environmental dominion look like a wild fantasy. Agriculture was a continual struggle. Wars and other violent skirmishes between tribes and nations were frequent (note too that most scholars date this text to a period of Babylonian domination, after Babylon destroyed Jerusalem and exiled many of its inhabitants—not a time of dominion). Famines and droughts often caused food shortages, sickness, starvation, and death. Life expectancy was in the thirties, and infant mortality rates were very high. It is estimated that a mother needed to have six babies in order to raise two to adulthood. The fragility and vulnerability of human life was an ever-present reality.

Read sympathetically, in light of a historical context in which humans are anything but godlike kings of creation, we can appreciate how the first creation story in Genesis might even have offered an escape from the exigencies of everyday life, a story world that imagines an original distant time of security and control.

As mentioned earlier, there is only one other biblical text, Psalm 8, that serves our modern notion of human godlikeness and dominion over creation. After recalling cosmic language from the early stages of creation in Genesis 1 ("heavens," "moon," "stars"), this hymn zeroes in on the creation of humans:

> You made them little less than God
> and crowned them with glory and majesty.
> You made them to rule over the works of your hands;
> you put everything under their feet. (8:5–6)

This poem amplifies the godlikeness and dominion of humans described in Genesis 1. Being made in the image of God means being made "a little lower than God" (or "gods"—'elohim is both a proper name and a plural noun). Godhood is then elaborated through a scene of coronation, ascribing humankind with "glory" (kavod) and "majesty" (hadar), terms often used in reference to God. Ostensibly a hymn of praise to God, this psalm serves also to glorify the godlike sovereignty of humankind as the creator's pièce de résistance.

But that is pretty much all there is. There are no other biblical texts to be leveraged in the promotion of human exceptionalism and godlike dominion. All the more astounding, then, that they have gotten such tremendous traction in our world, especially since the rise of modern capitalism. Why is it that, as we in the West have become more powerful, more exploitative, and more prosperous, we have also become more and more attached to and dependent on this biblical fantasy of death-denying godlike dominion, stitched together with a few small threads teased out of the larger biblical corpus? Why hasn't this little Bible story we keep telling ourselves faded away, as something no longer needed? Perhaps to assuage our guilt over our actions or to deny the consequences? Perhaps also because, paradoxically, the more we have asserted our power and control over the rest of the natural world, the more insecure we have become about our own fragility within it?

Another question: What if this story had never found its way into our Bibles, so that Genesis had started instead with this next story?

◆

7

HUMUS BEING

IMMEDIATELY FOLLOWING the first creation story in Genesis, the text jumps straight into another one. As noted earlier, this second creation story is not only centuries older than the first; it also employs a very different vocabulary and literary style, uses a different name for the divine creator, and describes a different order of creation, beginning with a single human and then proceeding to plants, animals, sexual difference, and so on.

This story is also much narrower in scope than the first one. It attends to relationships as they emerge and develop between God, humans, animals, plants, and the earth itself. It is a humbler, more grounded story (literally, as we will soon see). As such it offers a very different imaginative space for conceiving an understanding of what it means to be a human creature in relation to the creator, to other creatures, and to the earth.

EARTHEN SPIRITUALITY

This story begins not with cosmic elements like heavens and earth, light and darkness, sun and moon, but with a stretch of ground yet to bring forth life. Here is the opening scene as we know it from the familiar King James Version.

> And every plant of the field before it was in the earth, and every herb of the field before it grew: for the LORD God had not caused it to rain upon the earth, and there was not a man to till the ground. But there went up a mist from the earth, and watered the whole face of the ground.
> And the LORD God formed man of the dust of the ground, and breathed into his nostrils the breath of life; and man became a living soul. And the LORD God planted a garden eastward in Eden; and there he put the man whom he had formed. (Genesis 2:5–8)

The first image is of a fecund earth, pregnant with potential life. The plants and grasses are still underground, waiting for the LORD God (*yhwh 'elohim*) to make rain, and waiting for "man," another life form yet to emerge, to help them grow. At the same time, water rises from the earth to wet the ground's face. Then God creates the human, first shaping some dust, or better soil, from the ground into some kind of anthropoid form, and then blowing into its nostrils the "breath of life." This divine breath animates the human-shaped lump of dirt into what the King James Version calls a "living soul."

Going deeper, questions begin to emerge about this familiar old translation. For one, is this first human really a male human, a "man"? The Hebrew word here is *ha'adam*, which is the generic word for the human (*'iš* and *'išah* are "man" and "woman"). Later in the story, after this first human is put to sleep and divided into female and male, the word will be used without the definite article (*ha*, "the"), as a proper name for Adam. But that's getting ahead of the story. Here it is better translated "the human," not yet male or female, or perhaps both.

This first human is both poetically and linguistically connected to the fertile ground from which it is formed.[1] As is the case in English, where the words "human" and "humility" derive from the same root as "humus," so here *ha'adam*, "the human," is literally connected to *ha'adamah*, "the ground" or "humus." For this reason, we might better translate this Hebrew word as "groundling" or, as feminist biblical scholar Phyllis Trible proposed, "earth creature."[2] The human comes from the humus. It is literally humble, that is, close to the ground, grounded. And it will eventually return to that ground, as the creator God will later explain: "By the sweat of your nose you will eat bread until your return to the ground [*ha'adamah*], for from it you were taken. For you are soil [*'afar*], and to soil you will return" (3:19).

This ground, moreover, is not some passive mass of dirt but an active character in the story. It is imagined as alive with agency and subjectivity. The subterranean wellspring quenches its "face" (*panah*), or, more literally, "makes the ground's face drink." And it awaits the arrival of the human to . . . "till" it? The word is *'avad*, which elsewhere most commonly means "serve" (as in serving God, other gods, or another superior). Perhaps that was unthinkable to the translators of the King James Version and many other Bibles, who took it figuratively to mean something more like tilling or working the land. A little later, moreover, this same ground will "open its mouth" to consume the blood of Abel, whom Cain murdered, and will refuse to let Cain "serve" it (Genesis 4:10–11). This ground has personality and agency. It eats and drinks. It is served by humans and sometimes refuses to be served by them.

When God breathes into the nose of this human-shaped lump of humus, it suscitates. What are we to imagine here? The King James Version says it "became a living soul," but that may be misleading. In this ancient biblical context, there is no notion of a "soul" in our modern sense of the term, as a kind of spirit or essence of selfhood that lives beyond the body. Nor, for that matter, is there any notion of an afterlife to which such a soul could go. That kind of soul and that kind of ultimate heavenly home for them is foreign to these scriptures and their ancient Near Eastern context.

The phrase translated "living soul" in the King James Version is *nefeš hayah* ("neh-fesh chay-yah"). *Hayah* means "living" or "alive"—as in the modern Hebrew expression *leḥayim,* "to life!" *Nefeš* is closely related to its verb form, *nafaš,* "breathe" or "gasp," which refers to life-giving breath and can also refer to the throat or windpipe that takes it in.[3] So we might translate *nefeš ḥayah* as something like "breathing aliveness" or "breathing life." Used for the breathing lives of nonhuman as well as human animals, it is the aliveness that begins at birth with one's first breath and continues until one's last, at which point the *nefeš* departs the body—that is, ceases to animate it—and the body returns to the ground from which it came.[4]

Again, we should not mistake this departing *nefeš* for a person's soul or essence leaving the body behind, either to be with God in heaven or to be reincarnated in a new body. *Nefeš* is breathing life. When it stops breathing, the *nefešless* body returns to the soil, from whence it came. Which is why so many biblical passages imagine death not as the self or soul transcending worldly existence and going to heaven but rather as going down to *Sheol,* "the pit," that is, buried in the ground. As the priest recites while marking one's forehead with ashes on Ash Wednesday, the beginning of Lent, "Remember that you are dust, and that to dust you shall return."

With all this in mind, and in the spirit of opening new imaginative spaces from inherited traditions, here is my translation of the same story we just read from the King James Version:

> Every field sprout was still in the earth, and every field grass was yet to spring up. For LORD God did not make rain on the earth, and there was no humus being to serve the humus. And groundwater rose from the earth, making the face of the humus drink. LORD God formed the humus being, soil from the humus, and breathed into its nostrils life breath. And the humus being was breathing life. And LORD God planted a garden in east Eden, and put the humus being whom he formed there.

Here then is a story of beginning in the midst of things. Earth is already present. Seedlings have not yet broken through its surface.

Groundwater wells up from the earth, and the face of the ground drinks it in, quenched muddy. Like the plants, the human ground-ling emerges from the soil. Formed from mud, it is animated into a breathing life when God blows life breath into its nostrils. The hu-man groundling is divinely inspired soil, spiritual dirt, intimately connected to the ground and as close to God as breath.

This sense of earth-creaturely ecological interdependence, of grounded humility, continues as other forms of life emerge. God plants a garden and places the human there to serve and keep it. Seeing that it isn't good for the human to be alone, God creates other animals from the ground, presumably just as the human had been formed and animated into a living being. When none of the animals seems right for the human, God puts it into a deep sleep, takes one rib (or "side," *selaʿ*) from it, patches the flesh, and forms a woman (*'išah*). So you could say that it is the woman who is created first; the leftover portion is the man (*'iš*).

As my retranslation of this story suggests, moreover, when we read biblical Hebrew less figuratively and more literally (e.g., "breath" instead of "spirit," "face" instead of "surface" or "presence," "drink" instead of "water"), we can better see how deeply rooted it is in the body and bodily experiences in the natural world. The ground has a face and is made to drink. The human is formed from it with nostrils (does it have anything else?), and God brings it to life by blowing life breath into those nostrils. The garden is served by the human. Our propensity to translate less literally and more figuratively alienates us from this body language. We lose its earthy fleshiness, attuned as it is to this-worldly embodiment.

Earth creatureliness: dirty spirituality, God-breathed earth, ani-mated by a force of life shared with all other earth creatures. Of the ground, from the ground, returning to the ground with the departure of one's last life breath. Here biblical myth and contemporary science agree: all of life on this planet comes from and returns to the ground. Every plant, animal, and human that has ever lived on this planet is now part of it, making its humus rich for new life to come. With the rare exceptions of Timothy Leary, Gene Roddenberry, and a few others whose remains were "buried" in outer space, Earth holds the remains of everything and everyone that has ever lived and breathed on it. The surface of our planet is a rich, vast compost pile.

GRASSLIKENESS

The dominion verse and its dominionist interpretations notwithstanding, the earthbound mortal spirituality we encounter in Genesis 2 is presumed throughout most of biblical tradition. As mentioned earlier, humans are, like other animals, breathing lives, animated by *ruaḥ*, "breath" or "wind," whose flesh returns to the ground when they exhale their last breath. This is where we get the expression "to give up the ghost," where "ghost" is another word for "spirit," from the Latin *spirare*, "breathe,"[5] as in that airy force of life that comes with your first breath and departs with your last.

In fact, much of our modern language for spirituality goes back to this animistic notion of breathing life. To "expire" is to breath out for the last time. To "conspire" is to breathe or whisper together with another. To be "inspired" is to be in-breathed, to take in the breath or spirit of another. In this ancient poetic anthropology, humans and other animals share a common life spirit: all are formed of ground, inspired into breathing life, and ultimately return to the ground, taking part in new lives to come.

I pick up no sense of existential terror in these ancient traditions, as there is in some of Becker's descriptions of the "terrifying" and "repugnant" reality of mortality. Why not? Were those who first told these stories too "primitive" to understand the depth of our modern existential mortality crisis? Perhaps instead it's because the ancient cultures in which these stories circulated were more closely attuned to and interdependent with their immediate local environment. They were in touch with the reality of human subsistence, to the web of interdependence that we are all part of. They were practiced in earth creatureliness.

GROUNDING RELATIONSHIPS

This sense of earth creaturely humility also involves human relationship with the land. I'm not talking about stewardship, caring for or
over the land as if it were a resource. That kind of stewardship is little
more than a kinder, gentler dominion. On the contrary, I mean a
human relationship with the land imagined as a living character with
inherent value who is in intimate relationship with other lives and
with the divine.

In the poetic imagination of many biblical texts, the land has
agency. It is a subject whose actions impinge on humankind and
vice versa. It drinks rainwater from the skies (Deuteronomy 11:11).[6]
It feeds and nourishes people and other animals (Leviticus 25:19). It
joins other nonhumans in lamenting the injustices and bloodshed
perpetrated by humans, who are in denial of the consequences of
their actions (Hosea 4:1–3; cf. Jeremiah 4:28, 12:4).

Indeed, the land can be defiled and polluted by human transgres-
sions like murder, for which it has no ritual means of cleansing or
expiation (Numbers 35:33–34). Under the weight of such violence,
the land staggers like a drunkard and sways like an old shack (Isaiah
24:20). If its human inhabitants continue to defile it with their hor-
rors, it will vomit them out, just like it has done to previous inhabitants (Leviticus 18:25–28, 20:22).

The land also takes Sabbaths. Every seventh year, it must be left
to rest, to lie fallow in order to be refreshed. And after seven times
seven Sabbath years, in the fiftieth year, there is a Jubilee. In that
year, land rest is accompanied by other acts of restorative justice: all
debts are cancelled, lost property is restored to former owners, and
the land is left alone, with people and animals eating only what it
gives them (Leviticus 25).

Indeed, Sabbath observance by humans, animals, and the land
is inextricably tied to social and environmental justice. Practicing
Sabbath is an act of resistance against more familiar transactional
modes of being, in which we attain wealth and power by our own
mastery. Sabbath says that one cannot earn or own any of creation,

which can and will go on without us. Within this context, as Walter Brueggemann has argued, land Sabbath in particular is the practice of remembering that the land is not an entitlement. On the contrary, permission to dwell is conditioned on the proper and just relationship of humans with it and within it.[7] As poet-farmer-activist Wendell Berry puts it, "These sabbaths ritualize an observance of . . . the limits of human control. Looking at their fallowed fields, the people are to be reminded that the land is theirs only by gift; it exists in its own right, and does not begin or end with any human purpose."[8]

Within this tradition and this ecotheological poetics, the land is not to be treated as a matter of entitlement or property. It is imagined as a member of creation, a subject of verbs—drinking, giving, resting, mourning, sometimes staggering, sometimes vomiting. God looked after it before the Israelites came to dwell in it (Deuteronomy 11:12). The land was there before humans lived on it and will be there after they are gone.

Indeed, the land's permanence is often set in contrast against human mortality and impermanence. As Psalm 90 puts it, when humans return to the soil, God simply sweeps them away.

> You return humanity to dust.
> You say, "Return, human child" . . .
> You sweep them away;
> they are a dream.
> They are like grass renewed at daybreak:
> at daybreak it renews and flourishes;
> at dusk it withers and dries up. (90:3, 5–6)

Psalm 103 likewise reflects on the fleeting quality of human life in terms of dust and grass:

> For [God] knows our form,
> remembers that we are soil.
> Humans—their days are like grass.

Like a blossom of the field it flourishes;
when the wind blows over it, it is gone,
and its place remembers nothing of it. (103:14–15)

So much for being created like gods, subduing and having dominion over the rest of creation. In these images, we humans are the ones underfoot, briefly green and blossoming before withering or being swept away and forgotten.[9] A nightmare for a transhumanist, but a thing of wonder for the psalmist.

This biblical poetics of earth creatureliness speaks from an ecological perspective that understands the intimate relationship between *'adam* and *'adamah*, human and humus, groundling and ground, earth creature and earth. It understands that humility is about being close to the ground. To be humbled is to be brought low, brought back down from our delusions of godlike dominion, to come to terms with what is most real, namely our earth creatureliness.[10] Why do we so often loathe such humbling experiences as humiliating rather than welcoming them as grounding?

8

NO HOPE WITHOUT GRIEF

O NE OF MY FAVORITE spots near our house in Denver, Colorado, is a small pond called Duck Lake that sits just behind the Denver Zoo in City Park. In the middle of it is a tiny island of cottonwood trees that is a favorite nesting site for double-crested cormorants. They've been coming here for almost a century, ever since a half dozen of them were imported from a nearby lake to settle in the trees that the city had recently planted in what had been shortgrass prairie land for millennia.

Every spring, around March, they return to nest and give birth. The bare twisting branches of the island's dozen or so trees, many of them long dead, bend and sway under nearly two hundred round, clumpy nests, each with a slender, black, almost prehistoric looking mother perched vigilantly over it. The fathers fly low over the water and lakeshore in search of twigs, which they bring back home one at a time. To get back up to the high nests, they beat their wings hard, picking up speed while circling the island before swooping up to their partners. Sometimes a twig is too heavy or awkwardly shaped to get enough lift, and the bird gives up, returning to the water to reassess. Somehow they never cross paths, let alone collide in midair.

The mother is the main builder in each family, though the father helps. She places the heavier, coarser sticks on the exterior walls for structure, and lines the inside with softer materials. What a wonder of innate architectural instinct. What a remarkable aptitude for creating space for flourishing.

They're known to be social, even gregarious birds, talking to one another in a low, guttural cooing that sounds to me like the purring of a big cat. They seem perfectly comfortable sharing space with other creatures, including the night herons and geese fishing in the little lake around them.

PANDEMIC FRAGILITY

When the cormorants arrived and settled atop their familiar cottonwoods in early March of 2020, I wonder if they noticed that something was different. There were no chatty kids on skateboards on the nearby paths, no Frisbee golfers, no pairs of friends walking and talking, no young parents jogging behind strollers. The park, like the heavily trafficked streets around it, were ghostly silent and empty.

The world was in the early throes of COVID-19, what we were then still calling "the novel coronavirus pandemic." The numbers of new cases and deaths in the United States were growing exponentially and were expected to continue well into the summer. Perhaps, some were saying, much longer. The mayors of large cities were ordering residents to "shelter in place," a command used up till then primarily in active shooter scenarios and war zones. Indeed, many national and world leaders were beginning to describe the pandemic as a war.

Already back then, the responses of most Americans were spinning out in two opposite but equally insane directions. On the one hand, many were in nearly complete denial as to the serious threat and potentially dire consequences of the virus. They insisted, along with then president Donald Trump, that it would all soon pass on its own, probably with the warming spring weather. Contrary to the healthcare professionals and infectious disease researchers who were on the front lines, they were declaring that the United States was well prepared to handle it. And that the economy, which was already in full recession and suffering the highest unemployment rates in history, would bounce right back, probably in a matter of weeks if not days. Some even suggested that elderly people, who were more susceptible to the virus, should be willing to catch it and die so that younger generations could get back to work sooner and jumpstart the economy—to "die for the Dow."

On the other hand, many were descending into all-out panic. Within hours of the first news of the virus taking initial hold in American cities, stores had been emptied of disinfecting wipes, hand sanitizers, food essentials, and toilet paper. A week later, sporting goods stores and gun shops were selling out of firearms, ammunition, and survival gear. It was like a scene from *Night of the Living Dead*.

For many, even back then, it felt like the end of the world. In fact, doomsday predictions were spreading at least as fast as the virus. Some interpreted the virus as the Fourth Horseman of the Apocalypse from the biblical book of Revelation (chapter 6). He rides a pale green horse, his name is Death, and Hades follows behind him, wiping out a quarter of the world's human population in one fell swoop. Others were saying that the coronavirus was one of the seven plagues or "bowls of wrath" poured out by seven angels later in the book (chapter 16). The wildfires in Australia, they said, were another bowl. Once all seven have been poured out, some predicted, the Final Judgment would be upon us. For those with eyes to see and ears to hear, the end was at hand.

Although antithetical reactions, denial and doomsday dread were not only equally irrational but also equally dangerous. Both were essentially calls to inaction. Denial of the reality of the pandemic's threat to human health and to the economy contributed to our lack of preparedness when the crisis really began to escalate. Likewise, upgrading the crisis to the level of an apocalyptic doomsday deprived us of agency: it encouraged people to see the pandemic as a fulfillment of scriptures, God's will, part of a divine plan. After all, it has to get worse before it can get better. The best we can do is warn others to get right with God and hold tight till the trials and tribulations pass and Christ returns.

Each of these responses, which grew in popularity as the pandemic continued, also revealed something important, however unflattering, about us and our relationship with mortality. On the one hand, in the denial, we can recognize another facet of our incredibly tenacious ability to keep looking away from real threats to us as a species: how tightly it is often bound to nationalism. Other nations may perish, but we will soon bounce back, stronger than ever. Here, as in so many other cases in the United States, human exceptionalism was nearly synonymous with American exceptionalism, and both expressed our fundamental faith in our chosenness and special blessing.

On the other hand, our rapid escalation from the spread of a new virus to epidemic doomsday hysteria revealed how remarkably fragile our usual blithe ways of being in the world really are. The sense of security that makes it possible for most of us to sleep through most nights and wake up most mornings to face the day is remarkably brittle. It easily cracks open, revealing paralyzing anxieties and abysmal doomsday ideations.

8:46

A mile or so west of the nesting cormorants, there were new signs of another disease, one far more threatening than the pandemic, because it is in fact endemic to this nation: white racism. Many thousands of people in downtown Denver were joining many millions of people in hundreds of cities in the United States and around the world to protest police brutality and violence against Black people.

Images and stories from the events that ignited the protests that spring are now burned into our minds. On March 13 of 2020, just as the country was shutting down, we were learning about the gruesome killing in Louisville, Kentucky, of Breonna Taylor, a twenty-six-year-old Black woman who was shot eight times by three plainclothes police officers who had broken down her apartment door with a battering ram in pursuit of two drug dealers who did not live there and who had in fact already been arrested. Around the same time, a video was released showing the brutal murder in February of Ahmaud Arbery, a twenty-five-year-old Black man who was shot at point-blank range by self-appointed white vigilantes while jogging near his home in Brunswick, Georgia. Then, on May 25, a Minneapolis police officer murdered George Floyd, a forty-six-year-old unarmed Black man. A cell-phone video taken by then seventeen-year-old Darnella Frazier clearly showed the officer, Derek Chauvin, kneeling hard on Floyd's neck for almost nine minutes while surrounding officers stood by and did nothing. Floyd repeatedly begged for mercy, saying that he could not breathe, at one point crying out for his mother, until he lay lifeless on the street.

George Floyd, Breonna Taylor, and Ahmaud Arbery are among the most recent victims in the long history of police brutality and violence against Black people in the United States. White racism is a chronic disease. The United States was born with it and could very well die from it. It is deeply embedded in the foundations of this nation and its core institutions. This nation cannot seem to live without it and cannot continue for much longer with it.

The protests, which were largely peaceful, revealed just how far local and national governments will go to maintain law and order, even to the point of militarization. Riot police in full armor broke up marches with tear gas and rubber bullets. The National Guard was deployed in more than twenty states against its own people while they exercised their civil right to protest. Countless photos and videos in the news and social media showed people being tased or shoved to the ground while others choked on tear gas, their faces white with its powder residue. Among the most atrocious of scenes: military police using smoke canisters, pepper balls, and horses to drive peaceful protesters out of Lafayette Square in Washington, DC, in order to clear the way for President Trump to pose for photos of himself holding a Bible in front of St. John's Episcopal Church.

All of this has left many overwhelmed with anxiety, depression, and despair. For many people of color in America, especially for Black people, those experiences have been far more acute, exacerbated by centuries of systemic white racism in ways that I and other privileged white people cannot fully understand or imagine. "Each new death, each new example of an old injustice, renews our grief, sending little shock waves of sorrow," writes Marissa Evans in her essay "The Relentlessness of Black Grief."[1] Black people in the United States, suffering from police violence, economic disparities, and healthcare inequalities exacerbated by the pandemic, are in a "Black bereavement bubble—engorged by tears, intergenerational trauma, social distancing, Zoom-viewed homegoings, police killings, and inequities in the U.S. health-care system."

The toll is both emotional and physical. The intergenerational trauma, compounded over centuries of oppression, is carried in memories and stories as well as in bodies. As Resmaa Menakem explains in My Grandmother's Hands, a powerful book about racialized trauma, "white-body supremacy doesn't live in our thinking brains. It lives and breathes in our bodies," whose nervous systems carry "the widespread destruction of Black bodies," past and present, in a state of persistent trauma.[2] "Our very bodies house the unhealed dissonance and trauma of our ancestors."

Will the mutually intensifying catastrophes of the pandemic, whose effects will last for decades at least, and this most recent surfacing of white racism be the end of America as we know it?

Apocalypse: from the Greek apo-kalupto, "out of covering." An apocalypse is an unveiling or unmasking, a revelation of that which has been hidden. What is being unmasked now? Nothing less than the military police state that has enabled many of us—mostly white, wealthy, and male—to continue to live in the culture of denial that is American exceptionalism. In "XXX," a heartrending lament over the racial and economic inequalities of blessing in America, hip-hop artist Kendrick Lamar holds up a mirror, revealing us to ourselves in raw honesty. God bless you if you feel blessed, he begins, sarcastically. He goes on to mourn an American flag draped and dressed in munitions paraded down city blocks walled off by barricades and redlines. America, see how we have learned from you. See how we are reaping what we have sown. So much for our shining "city upon a hill," beacon of democracy, light unto the nations.

These are apocalyptic times. We are witnessing the revelation, the unmasking of American exceptionalism's deep dependence on white racism, violence, and exploitation. Will it be enough to break through the denial that sustains our delusions of chosenness and special blessing as a nation? Or will our deep, mostly subconscious drive to maintain the denial, to put the mask back on what has been unmasked, to veil what has been revealed, win out, leading to still further repressive violence? What will it take to break through denial to find some kind of hope?

Anger is part of it. Reflecting on his own experiences of helplessness in the face of dehumanizing treatments by white police officers over the course of his life, professor and theologian Willie Jennings reminds us that hope is not simply a feeling. Hope, he says, is a *discipline* that requires constant practice within the context of community. But there's still more to it: "what I have also learned is that living the discipline of hope in this racial world, in this white supremacist–infested country called the United States of America, requires *anger*."[3] Such anger, Jennings tells us, "is the engine that drives hope," keeping it focused on what needs to change now and why it cannot wait.

Jennings also believes that this kind of hopeful anger resonates with the righteous indignation of God. He understands that some of us may be uncomfortable with this linking of human anger with divine anger. We are well aware of the history of atrocities carried out by the righteously indignant against their enemies, whom they believe God hates as much as they do. To avoid such projections, Jennings insists on two conditions for claiming that one's own anger is also God's anger: first, it must be in response to the destruction of life, which means that it cannot turn into hatred, which blinds us to such destructiveness; and second, it must be shareable with other human beings.[4]

One of the most powerful expressions of this kind of righteous indignation was the 2020 YouTube performance by comedian Dave Chappelle entitled "8:46," for eight minutes and forty-six seconds, which was how long it was believed that Chauvin had kept his knee on George Floyd's neck (we later learned that it was actually nine minutes and twenty-nine seconds). Speaking before a live audience near his home in rural Ohio, this was no light comedy routine. Chappelle was visibly unsettled by recent events and inspired by the protests. At one point, his voice shaking, he declared to the hushed audience of people in face masks, "That you can *kneel on a man's neck for eight minutes and forty-six seconds*, and feel like you wouldn't get the wrath of God." To me, this is a prophetic moment, as Chappelle invited his audience, and us, to share in his anger, summoning divine wrath out of his own enraged bafflement that a human being could do such a thing to another human being. To be sure, such righteous anger in one context does not indemnify you from being the cause for it in another. So it is with Chappelle, who, in a later comedy special, made comments about transgender people that provoked righteous anger toward him. The kind of angry hope that Jennings is calling for is heard, I believe, in expressions of outrage like these, shared with others in response to hatred and the destruction of life.

FINDING A VOCABULARY FOR GRIEF

Hope also requires grief. That may sound illogical to some, for whom grieving means giving up on hope by giving in to loss and helplessness, admitting defeat. Not so. If anger drives hope, grief opens a path for it. To seek hope without moving through grief is to end in despair. This too is a lesson we can learn from biblical tradition, which not only allows for grief but privileges it. Although they don't get much play in the pulpit or Sunday school, many passages in the Bible dwell uncomfortably long in the valleys of pain and loss, resisting our anxious rush to ascend the mountaintops of hope.

Hebrew biblical tradition is especially well versed in grief, offering a deep imaginative pool of language to help us give voice to it. Behind the words "grief" and "grieve" in most English Bibles, there are thirteen different Hebrew words, with connotations ranging from physical injury to sickness, to mourning, to rage, to agitation, to sighing, to tottering unsteadily to and fro. The most common expressions speak to the ways emotional sadness and vexation are inseparable from embodied physical suffering in the face of loss.

The privileging of grief over and before any hope for restoration or healing is most powerfully expressed in the prophets. We sometimes imagine these speakers of truth to power as self-righteous haters, eager to see sinners suffer divine wrath. But they are better understood as poets who give voice to the reality of loss that their own people, whom they love and for whom they grieve, refuse to face. They grieve what their community denies, even as they strive to break through that denial.

Consider, for example, this remarkable oracle from the prophet Amos, lamenting the deep denial that was driving the most prosperous among his people to an early oblivion:

Woe! those who are at ease in Zion,
 those who feel secure on Mount Samaria,
 the designated heads of the peoples
 to whom the house of Israel goes . . .
those who put far away the day of calamity,
 and bring near a seat of violence . . .
those who lie on beds of ivory and stretch out on their couches,
 eating lambs from the flock and calves from the stall;
those who sing to the sound of the harp
 —like David they play with musical instruments;

those who drink wine from bowls,

   anointing themselves with the finest oils,

    And they do not grieve over the destruction of Joseph!

Therefore they will now be the first to go into exile,

   and the revelry of the loungers shall pass away. (Amos 6:1, 3–7)

Beginning with an exclamation of lament and grief—*hoy*, "Woe!" or "Alas!"—the poem unfolds in a series of verbal phrases describing the ill-gotten prosperity of the nation's elites, who bask in their wealth and security, putting calamity out of their minds, inviting violence. They lounge on expensive furniture. They stretch out. They eat fancy foods like lamb and veal. They sing and play with expensive instruments. They drink fine wine from bowls. They anoint themselves in opulence.

Then, very abruptly, the lavish cataloguing of their luxurious pastimes is interrupted by what they *do not* do but should be doing: "they do not grieve" (from ḥalah, "be sick") for the immanent ruin of their people. And so, the prophet declares, they will be the first to be carried away into exile.

Simultaneously pronouncing judgment and inviting sadness, Amos cries out in horror for those who recline in denial and do not (cannot? are unable to? refuse to?) grieve the ruin that is outside their high walls and doors. Though they are guilty, Amos nonetheless expresses grief over their imminent demise, about which they are in complete and total denial. Here as elsewhere, the prophet pronounces *judgment from the inside*, inviting "us" to look at ourselves, to stare at the wounds, to live into the pain, not as a path to healing but as reality in and of itself. In this way the poetry works to crack open the imperial ideology, which aims to consolidate wealth and power among an elite few, with an alternative way of seeing and being in the world based on justice and neighborliness. The prophet confronts ancient Israel's imperial ideology of special blessing and national exceptionalism with the realities of exploitation and violence. When that imperial delusion falls apart, the prophet confronts its denial of what is happening with grief, an invitation to deep sadness over what has been irreparably lost. Then, and only then, is it even possible for the prophet to confront the despair of an empire in ruins with hope for the possibility of healing and restoration.

Amos was calling out and grieving ancient *Israelite* exceptionalism, but his words speak powerfully to other forms of exceptionalism more familiar to us. Woe! to those who are at ease in America, who feel secure in gated communities, who stretch out on their couches, eating lamb and veal, drinking fine wine . . . Woe! to those who are at ease in the world today, who feel secure in prosperous countries, lounging in big cars and jets, drinking pricey bottled waters . . . who put far away the day of calamity.

EARTH MOURNS WHAT WE DENY

Searching for something that might break through the denial, these ancient poets conceived of an astonishing image, one that I believe also speaks to us: the earth itself grieving over the injustices and violence of its human inhabitants.

Recall how biblical tradition personifies the land, earth, and ground, imagining them as subjects whose own welfare is impinged on by human actions, and vice versa. In the prophets, this personification is elaborated in visions of the land grieving and mourning the unjust and ultimately self-destructive actions of its human inhabitants, even as they remain in denial.[5]

The prophet Jeremiah, for example, envisions the land mourning while his people pretend that God is blind to their ways: "How long will the land mourn and all the field grass wither from the evil of those who dwell in it? The animals and birds are swept away, for they [humans] said, 'He sees not'" (12:4).

Likewise, the prophet Joel imagines the ground mourning the impending doom while the people lie about in sleepy, drunken stupefaction: "Awake, drunkards, and weep," he declares (Joel 1:5). The people's stupefied denial stands in contrast against the grieving of the land itself: "The fields are devastated; the ground mourns. For grain is devastated, new wine is dried up, oil languishes" (1:10). These lines are dense with words for mourning and grief that also connote physical distress and the breakdown. The land and its fruits (grain, wine, oil) have collapsed in sorrow and desolation, even as its human inhabitants have yet to realize the woeful state into which they have already fallen.

Implicit in this poetics of the grieving land, moreover, is an intuitive understanding that *social justice* and *environmental justice* are inextricably intertwined. Thus Jeremiah envisions creation itself coming undone as a result of human injustice: "I looked at the earth, and behold, it was a formless void; and at the skies, and their light was gone" (4:23). This "formless void" (*tohu vabohu*) recalls the primordial chaos from which the world in all its complexity and diversity was created in Genesis, beginning with "let there be light." Here, then, is a vision of anti-creation, the return of creation to chaos. All is darkness as the mountains tremble and the hills bounce about. The land no longer bursts forth in fruitfulness. There is no vegetation, no animal life. Even the birds of the air are gone—an ominous image of ecological breakdown. Once-great cities lie in ruins. And, Jeremiah laments, "there is no human." In response, "the earth mourns, and the skies above go dark" (4:28).[6]

Notice, moreover, that Jeremiah is not so much imagining the end of the *world* but the end of the *human*. Although this vision of ecological chaos and mass extinction means the end of creation as we know it, the earth and skies survive. They will remain, having returned to their primordial state, even as they mourn. They were there before creation, and they will be there after.

There remains, moreover, the possibility of a new emergence, a new creation, from the primordial fecundity of earth. As Jeremiah's God says, "All the earth will be desolation, but I will not make a complete ending" (4:27).[7] Might we see this as a prophetic intimation toward the possibility of a posthuman creation? Still, the earth would go on without us, and would eventually forget us, as our last traces decompose into its soil, from which new life may emerge. These prophetic images seem to have no problem imagining that it was here before us and will be here long after us.

In its own creative way, these prophetic visions recognize what we often struggle to acknowledge, if we do not deny outright: there can be no social justice and well-being without ecological justice and well-being, and vice versa. These poetic visions of the earth and the ground mourning, languishing, tottering, and shaking with grief serve to break through our lack of acknowledgment and denial—to move the poet's human audiences to recognize the reality of their situation and to open themselves to a grief that can interrupt denial. As such they offer us resources for a poetics and vocabulary of grief over injustice and violence that is inseparable from climate grief.

9

SUBSISTENTIALISM

M Y EARLIEST MEMORIES of my father are of him in the woods. He knew every leaf and petal, every track and dropping. He could whistle almost any bird call perfectly. He could walk through thick undergrowth without making a sound, start a small fire in any weather, and read the life story of a tree in its branches and scars. He was a person of few words, and always seemed more at home in the forest than in the living room or back yard.

In my early years, our family lived on Forest Service ranger stations in Oregon and Washington, where Dad served as district ranger. He would sometimes be away for days at a time on firefighting crews. "Your father is out there," my mother once told me as I stood on the porch of our little house contemplating a fierce red-black glow in the distant sky.

As a young boy, I remember Mom putting me and my little sister Jenny in the car to go pick him up on the side of the road after a long day of deer hunting. I can picture him coming out of the trees at dusk and trudging down a steep rocky slope toward the car with his rifle in his right hand and a buck draped over his shoulders, oddly reminiscent of a shepherd carrying a stray sheep back to the flock. Later he and Mom dressed out the deer on the kitchen counter, carefully preserving it in filets and steaks that would be eaten by our family and our neighbors over the next several months.

When I was in the fourth grade, Dad's work took us to Anchorage, Alaska, where he served as forest supervisor of Chugach National Forest. Our house was several miles outside the city along the upper west side of the Rabbit Creek Valley, a watershed that runs from Rabbit Lake at the base of Suicide Peak in the Chugach Mountains through alpine foothills and empties into the Turnagain Arm, which flows to the Gulf of Alaska. It was less than a mile's hike through the woods from our house to the edge of Chugach State Park, whose nearly half a million acres border the seven million acres of Chugach National Forest. Had I wanted to, I could have walked out my front door and continued for about a hundred miles through the Chugach mountains to the city of Valdez, the end of the Alaska Pipeline, without crossing paths with a single other human.

Dad died after a long battle with amyotrophic lateral sclerosis (ALS), also known as Lou Gehrig's disease, a neurological disease that slowly kills off the motor neurons that control voluntary muscles. Sometimes the disease starts in the feet and legs. Dad's version started in the throat, so that he lost his ability to speak and swallow well early on but was able to walk and use his hands and arms for quite some time.

The last time he was in the woods was a few months before he died. He could no longer speak by then, but he could still walk and keep his balance, albeit with considerable effort. He and my sister Jenny had decided to spend a day deer hunting. They had separated, and Jenny was walking along a high wooded ridge, hoping to flush a deer down to Dad in the shallow valley below. Instead of a deer, a lone coyote came down into the clearing. Normally coyotes steer clear of people, but when it saw Dad, it continued walking slowly toward him. Dad speechlessly tried to shoo it away by clapping his hands and waving his arms. Weakened by the ALS, he stumbled and fell to the ground. The coyote kept coming, apparently unafraid. Still on the ground, Dad fired his rifle in the air. Thankfully, that sent the coyote running and summoned Jenny to help him to his feet and back home.

Later, he explained to me that that would be the last time he would ever go into the woods alone. Spelling out his words, letter by letter, by pointing to them on a laminated alphabet card that was his preferred communication technology, he said it was clear to him that the coyote knew he was sick and vulnerable. It probably would've attacked and killed him if he hadn't fired his rifle into the air. He wasn't speaking from fear or trauma; he was very matter-of-fact about it, knowing that his increasing weakness and vulnerability was now recognizable by other predators. It was completely natural.

Often the places I hiked and camped in Alaska as a teenager were home not only to coyotes, moose, and caribou but also to coastal brown bears and grizzly bears. I had encountered them in the woods on several occasions, but always at safe distances: a sow and two cubs fishing in a rushing river a couple hundred yards away; a big male feeding at sunrise on a gut pile left by moose hunters on the other side of a lake; tufts of wiry, reddish-blond hair caught in the brush near the tent; paw prints wider than truck tire tracks in the mud; steaming piles of scat speckled with bright red currants and purple blackberries; a half-eaten salmon in the middle of a trail.

By the time I was in high school, I'd become somewhat obsessed with bears and bear stories. One of my favorite books was an orange hardback entitled *Danger!* It was a collection of stories about near-death encounters with bears and other wild animals. My dad had friends who'd been attacked by brown bears and lived to tell about it. One, a wildlife photographer, was caught by a large brown that toyed with him like a cat with a mouse. The man played dead, curling up in a ball with his arms wrapped around his head. The bear repeatedly picked him up in his mouth, shook him like a rag doll, and dropped him, each time waiting to see if he'd try to get away. Eventually the bear took his prey for dead, or grew bored of the game, and roamed far enough away for the man to stagger up to a nearby road and flag down a car. The scars all over his head and upper arms from the bear's teeth bore witness to the terrifying experience.

I was both fascinated by and frightened of bears. They lived in my teenage imaginary like mythical monsters, lords of a wilderness netherworld. The idea of meeting one up close, face to face, was the stuff of both dreams and nightmares.

Then it happened. I'd just graduated high school, and my friend and I were celebrating with a day hike up McHugh Creek Trail, a short drive from Anchorage. It was one of my favorite hikes, ascending from the rocky shores of the Cook Inlet's Turnagain Arm through thick forests of cottonwood, aspen, and alder trees before opening onto the wind-swept foothills of the Chugach Mountains, where silver-green lichen, deep red bearberry leaves, and tiny purple wildflowers surrounded the lingering patches of melting snow.

We'd been hiking for about half an hour, peeling off layers of clothes as we climbed. Soon we'd reach the tree line and break through the dense alder brush onto an open hillside overlooking the tidewaters of the Cook Inlet about two thousand feet below. I was in the lead, breathing hard, my heart pounding in my ears.

My friend had brought along his dog, an energetic little mutt who scampered through the surrounding woods like a scout. We hadn't seen him for several minutes when he popped out of the woods and onto the trail about ten feet ahead and ran past me to his owner.

A split second later, right behind him, a huge brown bear crashed onto the trail. I don't know exactly how huge it was. Its shoulders were wider than the trail. Its head was nearly as broad, with a long, square snout and tiny black eyes. It probably weighed well over a thousand pounds. Standing, it would have been eight or nine feet tall.

The bear slowed to a stop about six feet in front of me, lifted slightly off its giant front paws, made a low, breathy woof at me, and turned off the trail, heading downhill through the brush.

I knew what to do in an encounter with a brown bear. I knew that these amazing animals can sprint at about thirty-five miles per hour, that they are likely to charge anything they don't immediately recognize and chase anything that runs away. I knew that if you meet one in the woods, the last thing you should do is turn and run.

Which is exactly what I did. Worse, I immediately tripped over myself and fell off the trail, directly in the bear's path. Lying face down, I heard the bear crashing through the brush behind me. Expecting to feel its claws grip into my back any second, I dragged myself back to my feet and ran blindly down the steep slope through the thorny brush. To my right I could see my friend running and tumbling down the trail. To my left was the bear, also heading downhill but angling away from me, disappearing into the woods. Apparently it was as eager to get away from me as I from it. But I was sure that it'd soon change its mind, get angry, and chase me down. I scrambled back onto the trail, and my friend, his dog, and I didn't look back or slow down till we'd reached the domestic safety of our car in the trailhead parking lot.

We made it home safe and sound, but it easily could have gone otherwise. More than a decade later, during a homecoming visit to Anchorage, another high school friend suggested we return to McHugh Creek Trail. I agreed, thinking it'd be a good way to face the lingering trauma from that long-ago encounter. That morning, as I was getting ready, my friend called and told me to check out the front page of the *Anchorage Daily News*. The day before, a seventy-seven-year-old woman and her forty-five-year-old son-in-law were attacked and killed on McHugh Creek Trail by a brown bear who was defending a nearby moose carcass that they hadn't realized was there. Needless to say, we decided to hike someplace else. Rather than overcoming my fears, I confirmed them as perfectly rational, appropriate, even natural.

I've never gotten over that encounter. My seconds-long brush with that brown bear demythologized the wild for me forever. I think what most overwhelmed and dizzied me was the sheer fact that it *moved*. No longer an object of my fascination, as in *Danger!*, it was the living, breathing, moving *subject* of my fear and awe, an other who could take my head off with a swipe of its paw, but who instead woofed and went another direction.

That bear shook something deep in my being. The familiar beauty of nature had suddenly shown itself as something other, something beyond me. No longer the denizen of my wilderness imaginary, that bear represented a real world in which I was vulnerable, finite, precariously tangential, edible. I was overwhelmed with the knowledge of my insignificance. I knew, in my little racing heart, the real possibility of being eaten. And I understood that that would be perfectly natural.

PRACTICES OF THE WILD

I often teach a college course called Religion and Ecology, which explores the ways religion shapes and is shaped by its environmental contexts. On the first day of class, I like to start by asking every student to share an experience they've had of "nature as wild," whatever that means to them. What happened? How did they feel? What changed, or didn't change? What might the story reveal about our different understandings of "nature" and "wild," and how we as humans relate to them?

One reason for starting this way, I have to admit, is that I get to share my bear story. But another and better reason is that it's a great way for my students and me to begin getting to know one another and building a sense of community. I still remember stories from years ago. There was the young woman who discovered that the loaf of Wonder Bread in the cupboard had been hollowed out by a colony of black ants. And there was the young man who described a face-to-face encounter with his pet cat, whose cold stare made him realize that it would eat him if he were smaller. For many, it was a moment of crossing an until-then invisible line from control and orientation into disorientation: straying off the trail in the woods; being pulled under by rapids or a powerful undertow; finding yourself overtaken by a thunderstorm; realizing a pack of stray dogs had started following you in the park; venturing beyond cell tower range. For others, it was a new perspective on what is daily under our very noses: the worms beneath the paving stones eating decaying plants and bugs; a raven tugging at the red flesh of a new roadkill as cars speed past; the climbing weeds choking out expensive perennials and ruining a newly painted fence.

Still another reason I like to start with this exercise is that it pushes us to think about the *constructedness* of our ideas of "nature" and "wild," along with other related ideas. As we share our stories, we begin to see more clearly how their meanings are built on a set of binary oppositions that, when scrutinized more carefully, don't quite hold: culture versus nature, artificial versus natural, domestic versus wild, human versus animal, order versus chaos, and so on. What is nature? That which is not culture. What is the wild? That which is not domesticated or civilized. What is human? That which is not animal. By means of such oppositions, we construct understandings of ourselves and our world.

This set of *anthropocentric* binaries, moreover, operates in parallel with the *androcentric* binaries that construct, maintain, and privilege male identity within heteronormative patriarchal culture: male versus female, masculine versus feminine, straight versus queer, and so on.[1] Likewise those binary oppositions that privilege the construct of whiteness and modern Western identity against other racial, ethnic, and cultural identities. All of these work to locate and secure a sense of self versus other, "us" versus "them."

Yet all these binary formulations of identity are inherently fragile, susceptible to deconstruction. The subject, the "I," depends on the objectification of the "other," the not-I and not-us, against which "I" define and secure my own selfhood. What, then, if the object does not oblige, does not stay put? As Luce Irigaray asks with regard to the fragility of masculine identity, "But what if the 'object' started to speak? Which also means to 'see,' etc. What disaggregation of the [male] subject would that entail?"[2] What happens when the other does not stay where I need it to stay, over against me, a kind of negative image of myself? In that moment, my sense of confidence in my own location, my own identity as a clearly defined and stable "I," suddenly becomes shaky, subject to disaggregation, that is, a kind of falling apart or meltdown of secure selfhood.

Which is what most of our experiences of "nature as wild" are about: they are moments when our inherited and largely unexamined ideas of nature, animality, and what it means to be human are disrupted and undermined. In such moments, "nature" is not being what I imagine it to be, indeed what I need it to be. It is no longer an object of beauty, or a subject of scientific research, or a natural resource over which I am steward. Suddenly I have become subject to it, not the other way around. It is as if the objectified other has started to speak, to see, etc. And in that moment I feel my own self disaggregating, coming apart, and being subjected to a larger reality that can and will ultimately overtake my little vulnerable selfhood. "Nature as wild" means nature as irreducible to my objectifications of it. Experiences of it are revelations of my constructed ideas of it, and of myself, and my deep dependence on those ideas.

Such revelations can be wonderful, terrifying, or both at the same time—"aweful," to use the older spelling of the word, which captures the experience of being overwhelmed by an otherness that is simultaneously fascinating and dreadful.[3] These revelations also, at least potentially, bring with them the possibility of personal and social transformation. They open us to new possibilities of relationship, hospitality, justice, grace, and community, even as they open us to the humbly awesome reality of our human condition, what Becker called the lived truth of creation: that we are part of and subject to a universal web of interconnection and interdependence—the biological, geological, and, yes, technological singularity. A singularity that is a vehicle not for human transcendence but for human *subscendence* into that from which we were born and to which we ultimately return.

This is what Gary Snyder describes as the food web, that is, the reality of eating and being eaten that is the most tangible, everyday epiphany of interbeing and interdependence. Recognizing and accepting our place within the food web is key to his call to "the practice of the wild," which is about getting in touch with our creatureliness within a "wild world that is innately and loosely orderly."[4] The practice of the wild opens us to the truth of the food web, namely:

There is no death that is not somebody's food, no life that is not somebody's death. . . . The shimmering food-chain, the food-web, is the scary, beautiful condition of the biosphere. . . . We look at eggs, apples, and stew. They are evidence of plenitude, excess, a great reproductive exuberance. Millions of grains of grass-seed that will become rice or flour, millions of codfish fry that will never, and must never, grow to maturity. Innumerable little seeds are sacrifices to the food-chain. A parsnip in the ground is a marvel of living chemistry, making sugars and flavors from earth, air, water. And if we do eat meat it is the life, the bounce, the swish, of a great alert being with keen ears and lovely eyes, with foursquare feet and a huge beating heart that we eat, let us not deceive ourselves.[5]

And we too are part of this shimmering web of interdependence. We will be food, as Snyder reminds us, whether we are eaten quickly by a bear while still warm or very, very slowly, by critters in the cold ground. As will the buildings and playgrounds and tools we have made. This is the true singularity. And it's not just near. It's here.

SUBSISTENCE PRECEDES ESSENCE

Many find such wisdom disturbing, a dreadful reminder of the human condition. Certainly it is what the transhumanists desperately want to transcend. And recall how Becker described it: "the terror" of an "impossible situation," an "excruciating" and "terrifying dilemma," a "nightmare of loneliness in creation," a "grotesque fate," "hopelessly" in nature, which "mocks us" while our "poets live in torture."

I heard that novelist Joyce Carol Oates once said that the root of all horror is the fear of being eaten. The vampires and zombies that populate so many of our horror stories today testify to that. Still, if it's true, then horror is a distinctly modern Western phenomenon. For, as we have seen, the history of the modern West has been obsessed with denying our animal mortality—driven, that is, by the fear of dying and being eaten (not necessarily in that order). And that drive to transcend what is believed to be a tragically flawed world, as Snyder well understands, "leads to a disgust with self, with humanity, and with nature," and ends up "doing more damage to the planet (and human psyches) than the pain and suffering that is in the existential conditions they seek to transcend."[6]

Against such existential panic, the practice of the wild calls us back to what I propose we call *subsistentialism*. To *exist*, from the Latin *existere*, is to "stand out," to put oneself forth in the world. Jean-Paul Sartre, speaking for the then new movement of existentialism, declared that "existence precedes essence." A person is nothing to begin with, and "will not be anything" except "that which he makes of himself . . . man is, before all else, something which propels itself towards a future and is aware that it is doing so. Man is, indeed, a project which possesses a subjective life, instead of being a kind of moss, or a fungus or a cauliflower. Before that projection of the self," that act of standing out, "nothing exists."[7]

Such heroic self-making is rarely if ever fully realized, even momentarily. No wonder, then, that most of us resonate more with "existential crisis" than we do with the valorous "existential triumph" envisioned here as a kind of independent, fully rational self-making, standing out, being exceptional. An existential crisis is about coming to terms with our ultimately not outstanding, unexceptional return to earth.[8]

Alongside whatever existential aspirations we may have, we need to embrace the reality of subsistence. If existence is about standing out and stepping forth, asserting oneself over and out of the world of moss and fungus and cauliflower, then subsistence is about standing under and within it, allowing oneself to be subjected to and part of it. Subsistence precedes essence.

When the word "subsistentialism" first came to me, I foolishly imagined that perhaps I was the first to use it. Which would have been, ironically, pretty outstanding. Such was not the case, however. That said, those who have used it before me have tended to give it a negative connotation. It comes with an implicit "mere" in front of it. It is about "mere subsistence," that is, "barely getting by." This reveals much about the disdain and condescension we moderns carry, however subconsciously, toward people and cultures that practice subsistence living. They appear to us to have given up on any greater ambitions or aspirations to stand out. They seem to us to have succumbed to some kind of lowest common denominator of animal survival.

The practice of the wild requires a return to subsistential reality. It calls on us to follow a path of mindful subsistence. It is fundamentally earth creaturely. It invites us to remember and embrace the lived truth of creation, which is the fundamental, literally humbling connection between human and humus. Remember that you are soil and that to soil you will return.

A subsistentialist practice of the wild can begin very easily, almost inadvertently. You might simply saunter off a familiar trail, down a slope and into a watershed, discovering a vast microcosm of living and nonliving beings worth lifetimes of attention in the small creek that runs down the middle. Or you might create new rituals and practices for eating more mindfully, recognizing that this most fundamental human activity can be the means of becoming aware of our subsistential reality in the "shimmering food-chain," which is "the scary, beautiful condition of the biosphere," an ever-available revelation of the truth of impermanence and interdependence.

BIBLICAL ABORIGINAL

Snyder also invites us to learn the practice of the wild from indigenous religions, such as the Australian Aborigines and the Ainu of Northern Japan. In these cultures, religious beliefs and practices are intimately related to, indeed inseparable from, the environments in which they emerged and continue to be maintained. In such contexts, modern Western distinctions like "culture" versus "nature," "human" versus "animal," and "domestic" versus "wild" lose their common sense. The sacred places these cultures revere and protect from generation to generation "are gates through which one can—it would be said—more easily be touched by a larger-than-human, larger-than-personal, view."[9]

Part of my interest in rereading the Hebrew scriptures in the previous chapters has been to rediscover remnants of ancient Israelite and Near Eastern indigenous religious beliefs and practices therein. These, I believe, are traces of aboriginal roots that survive in the scriptural traditions of Judaism and Christianity. To be sure, these traces take work to tease out, as they have been subsumed under a few biblical verses better suited to the religion of godlike dominion and human exceptionalism that has fueled modern Christian and post-Christian capitalist imperialism. Indeed, the entire biblical canon has been so completely claimed and embraced by the modern West as its own that most people think of it not only as part of the "Western canon" but actually as Western literature. It is not. As I have tried to show, much of it is in fact closer to the kinds of indigenous religious beliefs and practices that the modern West has denigrated as "primitive" or "savage."

I have teased out these texts, entangled as they are with other biblical strands that have been roped into claims of godlike dominion and human exceptionalism, the religion of the Anthropocene, as resources that might help us through our denial of death as a species and the immortality vehicles it fuels.

Against the dominionist strain, I hope I have shown how these traditions give voice to a subsistentialist theology and spirituality of earth creatureliness. At the core of this perspective is the humble recognition of an intimate relationship between the human and the humus, the earth creature and the earth. That we are, poetically and literally, inspired mud, animate soil. It acknowledges the ultimate impermanence of subsistence, that our coming and going is part of a larger web of constant change. Indeed, the wonder and awe we feel when we are surprised by something new—a birth, a sprout, a bloom, a rush of wind, a tornado—is bound up with its fleetingness.

This biblical earth creatureliness attests to a religious worldview that is rooted in indigenous cultural practices of subsistence in and with the land and other creatures. For centuries it has been denigrated or dismissed as a primitive embarrassment—the vestige of a crude and primitive religiosity that modern Christianity left behind long ago. When we have not been able to translate it away into more figurative expressions, or to play it down as mere poetry, we have simply ignored it, building a modern faith in dominion and human exceptionalism better suited to our interests in extraction and infinite growth.

As we approach the endgame for that religion, the religion of the Anthropocene, perhaps we can revisit and reclaim these surviving vestiges of biblical aboriginality, which are neither modern nor Western. Together with the lessons of other indigenous religious ideas and practices, I hope that they can help open up places in our too familiar daily lives where we might step off the trail and into the wild.

EPILOGUE
Kids These Days

S OON, ALL OF THIS WILL BE GONE." Our daughter Sophie was four when she made that comment, smiling nonchalantly from her car seat. That was almost twenty-five years ago. She's now a graduate student in divinity school and plans to be ordained as a Presbyterian minister.

"I think a lot about that story," she told me recently. She doesn't remember it directly, but she grew up hearing her parents tell it. Although the idea that "all this will be gone" apparently didn't frighten her when she was four, it wasn't long before it began to. "I think I was around seven when I learned that the sun is a star that will someday die. I don't know if I learned it in school or in some book or conversation. But it really hit me. I couldn't sleep. I remember you coming into my bedroom to see what was wrong. I told you about it, and you were like, 'Yeah, that's true and that's a thing that will happen. But it won't happen until after your great-great-grandchildren's great-great-grandchildren's great-great-grandchildren's grandchildren have come and gone.'

"I've thought about that answer lately. It's a funny way to put it. You were saying it would happen to people connected to me, related to me, people that I should somehow still care about. But still it calmed me down because it put so much distance between me and the end.

"But then I think about kids these days, and I can't imagine what it's like to grow up knowing that there's this catastrophe that they're

inheriting but had no part in creating. And it's not countless generations away. It could be within their generation. And they're so angry.
But no matter how many protests, no matter how many impassioned
speeches, they don't seem to be getting through. So the anger grows."

Sophie is so right. There is a rising fury among young people today. I see it in the growing numbers of them leading climate justice
protests and strikes. Above all, I feel it in the searing eyes, the fur-
rowed brow, and the quivering but stern voice of one of their fiercest
young prophetic voices, Greta Thunberg. "How *dare* you," she began
her address at the 2019 United Nations Climate Action Summit.

> You are failing us, but young people are starting to understand
> your betrayal. . . . You have stolen my dreams and my childhood
> with your empty words. And yet I'm one of the lucky ones. People
> are suffering. People are dying. Entire ecosystems are collapsing.
> We are in the beginning of a mass extinction, and all you can
> talk about is money and fairy tales of eternal economic growth.
> How dare you![1]

For decades, she continues, we have had all the scientific evidence
we've needed to take urgent and drastic action to try and address the
climate crisis. Yet there are no real solutions on the horizon, only ones
that can be fairly easily integrated into plans for "eternal economic
growth." And now it may well be too late. "You say you hear us and
that you understand the urgency. But no matter how sad and angry
I am, I do not want to believe that. Because if you really understood
the situation and still kept on failing to act, then you would be evil."

And we, the elder generations she is addressing, do not know what
to do with the crystal clear, truth-to-power rage and anguish that she,
along with so many others, needs us to hear. What I mostly see is how
quickly we shift the focus away from her hard words and onto her
remarkable courage and exceptional talents as an individual. We ap-
plaud and celebrate her growing number of honors and awards. We buy
the special issue of *Time* with her on the cover as "Person of the Year."

Isn't she amazing? And so young! Gives me hope for the future! Or we skip over her anger and jump ahead to more feasible action items— more green jobs, wind power, reduced packaging, all-electric automobile fleets by 2050. We are as well-meaning as we are condescending.

But when I go back and rewatch her speeches, what hits me most of all is the anger and grief over our failure. A failure for which we will never be able to atone. There is no making up for it. "You have stolen my dreams and my childhood." Before I am moved to action, which is urgently necessary whether or not I believe our climate crisis can be slowed or even reversed, I am being asked to sit uncomfortably with this failure, indeed this betrayal.

This is what truly prophetic voices do for us. They remind us that any real hope must first face and grieve the realities of our surroundings, the beds we have made for ourselves—or rather, in this case, for our children. Otherwise what we call hope is nothing more than another form of denial, another immortality vehicle.

Greta Thunberg and her peers are the prophets of our day. We need their anger, their rage. It is the voice of righteous indignation. Recall the two conditions Willie Jennings identified as necessary for claiming righteous indignation: it must be a response to the destruction of life, which prevents it from turning into life-destroying hatred, and it must be shareable with other human beings. Check, and check. Such anger can be, as Jennings puts it, "the engine that drives hope," attuning us to what needs to change most urgently.

These young prophets are also creating space to grieve and inviting us to share in that grief. There can be no hope without grief. We have to sit with it, not as a stage to pass through in order to get to hope, but for its own sake. We must sit in and with the ruins, the ashes of our aftermath.

These emerging prophetic voices are also pressing us to recognize the deep connections between environmental justice and social justice, in particular the ways that our deep commitments to infinite economic growth through extraction generate tremendous suffering and violence for the most vulnerable among us—a clear manifestation of how denial-driven exceptionalism unfolds in environmental racism and environmental classism. Climate activists like Isra Hirsi, a young Black Muslim woman who founded US Youth Climate Strike, are making powerfully clear that people of color suffer disproportionately due to climate change, even as they call on the climate movement to become more diverse and to lift up more underrepresented voices. Hirsi's own experiences in what is still a majority-white youth movement empower her "to make sure that those that are disproportionately affected by climate change be at the forefront of the issue, advocating for ourselves and our communities."[2]

A growing number of young voices are also drawing our attention to the pain and displacement that Indigenous peoples undergo as a result of economic policies and practices driven by faith in infinite growth through environmental extraction. At the same time, in what I receive as acts of breathtaking grace, some are also teaching us new ways of seeing and being human in the world based on the traditions of their own cultures. Xiye Bastida, for example, is bringing wisdom from the Otomi-Toltec nation, the indigenous culture of Mexico in which she was raised, to mainstream climate justice activism. Foundational to her indigenous ecology and cosmology is an understanding of *reciprocity* among living and nonliving beings and between humankind and the earth within larger networks of interdependence and responsibility. As we know from indigenous cultures around the world, such an understanding refuses to think of nonhuman beings and things as resources, instead seeing them as having intrinsic or inherent value, in and of themselves. "We need to shift the narrative," Bastida says, "to weave personal stories into data," shaping them into narratives that can be integrated into mainstream culture.[3] What changes, for example, when we talk about water not as "natural resource" but as "sacred element"? Bastida and other prophetic voices are helping us recognize that climate justice is not only about economic and environmental policies; it is about creating new spaces in which to reimagine ourselves and our place in the world.

This book is my modest attempt to answer the call of Bastida, Hirsi, Thunberg, and so many others, to join the marches and the strikes, and also to join the conversation about how to shift the narrative, to make space for imagining new possibilities and rediscovering ancient ones, and in the process to find hope that can break through the denial. What I have tried to bring to this conversation is some insight into how we got to this state of denial, how religion has so powerfully inspired, indeed ordained this denial, and also how religion might help us break through it, developing an alternative, palliative understanding that is compatible with the reality of human finitude, the lived truth of creation, and a finite future for our species.

Whether we have a generation, or seven generations, or even more. Whether there is still time before it's too late, or it is already too late. What matters most when time becomes short is always what matters most.

ACKNOWLEDGMENTS

I T TOOK ME several years to find my way to this book. There were quite a few false starts, a couple of which I didn't abandon for several months and way too many pages. I am deeply grateful for friends, colleagues, and students who stayed with me in the process. Jon Adams, April Favara, Ed Gemerchak, Michael Hemenway, Tod Linafelt, and Eric Pellish read drafts of the whole thing and offered invaluable comments, corrections, and recommendations for revision. Brian Murphy joined me in a months'-long staged writing race through the darkest year of the COVID-19 pandemic. The rules were simple, prioritizing quantity over quality: whoever wrote the fewest words each week bought the drinks, which we enjoyed in parks and backyards while discussing progress on our projects (his was a dissertation on urban river science). Several other friends read parts of drafts and engaged with me in conversations that helped me figure out what it was I was actually trying to do here. Thanks especially to Joy Bostic, Walter Brueggemann, David Carr, Bill Deal, Sarah Gridley, Richard Nodell, Brent Plate, Kathleen Wells, and Sally Wile for those engagements.

It's been so good to work again with Amy Caldwell, who was also my editor on *Roadside Religion* way back when. She truly is one of the best editors I know—deeply thoughtful, incredibly smart, steadfast, and patient. I'm also grateful to my agent, Don Fehr, for helping me shape a book idea and proposal that turned out to be such a good match for Amy and Beacon.

Thanks as well for vital support from university colleagues, especially Dean Joy Ward and the Expanding Horizons Initiative; my department chair, Justine Howe; and our department administrator, Lauren Gallitto.

I do a lot of my writing in diners and cafés, and I'm happy to acknowledge my most frequented ones here. In Cleveland: Tommy's, Big Al's, Yours Truly, and Luna. In Denver: St. Mark's, Cake Crumb, The French Press, The Corner Beet, and Logan House. I'm grateful as well for City Park Denver, in the shade of whose trees I spent countless hours writing during the many shutdown months of the pandemic, and for the Cleveland Metroparks, especially the South Chagrin Reservation, on whose trails I walked my dog and my way through early conceptions of this book.

I'm incredibly lucky to have a family that not only encourages me but also challenges me to learn and grow in my thinking and writing. This book is so much better for their suggestions, insights, and critical feedback. Clover, Sophie, Seth, and Gerri, you are my best critics and ideal readers. I love you.

Finally, my deepest thanks go to the students in my course Religion and Ecology, to whom I dedicate this book. Over the past three years, students in this course read and commented on my work at every stage, from drafts of proposals to drafts of manuscripts. They did so with interest, insight, grace, and enthusiasm. There is not a paragraph in this book that does not bear their influence.

NOTES

INTRODUCTION WITH PLAYLIST

1. An excellent account of the science behind the potential for a sixth extinction is Elizabeth Kolbert's *The Sixth Extinction: An Unnatural History* (New York: Henry Holt, 2014). For a fascinating and provocative history of the idea of extinction, see Thomas Moynahan's *X-Risk: How Humanity Discovered Its Own Extinction* (Falmouth, UK: Urbanomic, 2020). Moynihan focuses on the modern conception of extinction as "the end of sense," that is, "the irreversible end of moral activity and sapient value" in the cosmos (42), which he argues was not possible before the Enlightenment's understanding of "ourselves as a biological species within a desacralized cosmos" (8). He rightly distinguishes this concept from earlier religious forms of apocalyptic thought, which offer something more like a "sense of an ending" or "observation of the end" (33). That said, I will argue that other religious perspectives do in fact conceive of extinction in ways kindred to modern conceptions, rooted as they are in environmental contexts of subsistence that put them in touch with human extinguishability in ways that feed into the modern conception that Moynihan is historicizing.

2. "Anthropocene" was coined by P. J. Crutzen and E. F. Stoermer, "The 'Anthropocene,'" *IGBP Newsletter* 41 (2000): 17–18, "to emphasize the central role of mankind in geology and ecology." For a discussion of the history of the term in environmental science and the debate about whether it should be categorized as a geological epoch distinct from the Holocene, see Richard T. Corlett, "The Anthropocene Concept in Ecology and Conservation," *Trends in Ecology & Evolution* 30.1 (2015); Erle C. Ellis, "Anthropogenic Transformation of the Terrestrial Biosphere," *Philosophical Transactions of the Royal Society* A 369 (2011): 1010–35; and esp. Erle C. Ellis, *Anthropocene: A Very Short Introduction* (Oxford: Oxford University Press, 2018), 1–74.

3. Ellis, *Anthropocene*, 72–74.

4. Gary Snyder, *The Practice of the Wild: Essays* (San Francisco: North Point Press, 1990).

5. I have unpacked this understanding of religion as re-reading more fully in "Opening: Cracking the Binding," in Timothy K. Beal and David M. Gunn, eds., *Reading Bibles, Writing Bodies: Identity and The Book* (London: Routledge, 1996), 1–12; and in Timothy Beal, *The Rise and Fall of the Bible: The Unexpected History of an Accidental Book* (New York: Houghton Mifflin Harcourt, 2011), 180–96.

6. Lynn White Jr., "The Historical Roots of Our Ecologic Crisis," *Science* 155 (1967): 1207. I am not arguing for or against White's larger argument about the extent to which Christian scriptural and theological tradition is responsible for our ecological crisis. His thesis is more complex than many of its proponents and detractors have recognized, arguing that the roots of this crisis are found in Christian dominionism combined with the merging of science and technology in the medieval and early modern Christian West. See the various positions and responses in Todd LeVasseur and Anna Peterson, eds., *Religion and Ecological Crisis: The "Lynn White Thesis" at Fifty* (New York: Routledge, 2017). For critical perspectives from Hebrew biblical scholars on the "Lynn White Thesis," see also Gene M. Tucker, "Rain on a Land Where No One Lives: The Hebrew Bible on the Environment," *Journal of Biblical Literature* 116.1 (1997): 3–17; and the summary of earlier nuanced interpretations of the Hebrew biblical tradition in Jeremy Cohen, *"Be Fertile and Increase, Fill the Earth and Master It": The Ancient and Medieval Career of a Biblical Text* (Ithaca, NY: Cornell University Press, 1989), 15–19.

7. Sallie McFague, "Falling in Love with God and the World: Some Reflections on the Doctrine of God," *Ecumenical Review* 65 (2013): 19; see also her early and highly influential *The Body of God: An Ecological Theology* (Minneapolis: Fortress Press, 1993), which develops out of early theoretical work on the fundamentally metaphorical character of all theological discourse (esp. *Metaphorical Theology: Models of God in Religious Language* [Minneapolis: Fortress Press, 1982]).

8. Dorothy Dean, "'At Home on the Earth': Toward a Theology of Human Non-Exceptionalism," *Journal for the Study of Religion, Nature & Culture* 14.4 (2020): 480–95, which develops this theological anthropology through an interfacing of the theology of McFague and the phenomenology of Maurice Merleau-Ponty. "The flesh is the means by which the human and world are able to interact; participation in the flesh of the world is what makes it possible for the body to touch and see objects" (487, 488). I consider Dean's work toward a "fleshy theology," which I discovered very late in the process of finishing this book, to be some of the most promising in the field of constructive Christian ecotheology.

9. The playlist can be found at https://open.spotify.com/playlist/1ReaL 2Hoe74XiPiq4Hhoi4?si=sV5_ZYnnQLWx6JrSFNMgvg.

10. Walter Brueggemann, *Reality, Grief, Hope: Three Urgent Prophetic Tasks* (Grand Rapids, MI: Eerdmans, 2014). Brueggemann is referring to the ancient Israelite empire of Solomon, but also by extension to the contemporary regime of imperial technological military consumerism.

11. Anthony de Mello, *Awareness: The Perils and Opportunities of Reality*, ed. J. Francis Stroud (New York: Doubleday, 1992), 169.

1: SOON, ALL OF THIS WILL BE GONE

1. The following summary of missed opportunities to slow or reverse global warming is indebted to Nathaniel Rich's compelling and thoroughly researched essay "Losing Earth: The Decade We Almost Stopped Climate Change," *New York Times Magazine*, August 1, 2018, https://www.nytimes.com/interactive/2018/08/01/magazine/climate-change-losing-earth.html. Powerfully illustrated by George Steinmetz, Rich's essay chronicles the decade or so, from the late 1970s to the late '80s, during which it would still have been possible to dramatically decrease carbon emissions and slow or even stop global warming.

2. Philip Shabecoff, "Global Warming Has Begun, Expert Tells Senate," *New York Times*, June 24, 1988.

3. This book is not an argument for the reality of anthropogenic global warming and related environmental crises; the scientific evidence is beyond any reasonable doubt. Helpful, up-to-date information is available at https://climate.nasa.gov. For me, one of the clearest indicators of dramatic global warming since the 1980s is the year-to-year ratio of record-high temperatures to record-low temperatures. In a stable climate situation, the number of record highs around the world in a given year would match the number of record lows that year, yielding a roughly one-to-one ratio of highs to lows. Over the past three decades, by contrast, that ratio has tipped further and further toward the highs, to the point now that record highs outnumber record lows by about two-to-one. In 2018, for example, there were about 28,000 record highs and about 14,000 record lows. The year 2019 was the second-hottest on record, losing only to 2016, and by a mere seven-hundredths of one degree Fahrenheit. The year 2020, which was unprecedented in so many ways (including how frequently the word "unprecedented" was used to describe it), essentially tied with 2016.

4. Gro Harlem Brundtland et al., *Environment and Development Challenges: The Imperative to Act*, Blue Planet Prize report (Tokyo: Asahi Glass Foundation, February 20, 2012), https://www.af-info.or.jp/en/blueplanet/assets/pdf/bpplaureates/2012jp_fp_en.pdf.

5. See esp. the work of Hans-George Gadamer, *Truth and Method*, 2nd rev. ed., trans. Garrett Barden and John Cumming; revised and translated by Joel Weinsheimer and Donald G. Marshall (New York: Crossroad, 1993), first published in 1960 as *Warheit und Methode*. Gadamer effectively

transformed hermeneutics into the science of understanding. For an accessible introduction to Gadamer's work, see William E. Deal and Timothy Beal, "Gadamer, Hans-Georg," in *Theory for Religious Studies* (New York: Routledge, 2004).

6. The earliest use of the phrase "human exceptionalism" that I can find in the context of environmental studies, which borrowed it from anthropology, is in S. Z. Klausner, *On Man and His Environment* (San Francisco: Jossey-Bass, 1971), 180: "The doctrine of human exceptionalism, whether divine or rationally based, is a paradigm that is clearly no longer satisfactory for explaining either man's transactions with the environment or man's transactions with his fellow man." He was arguing that environmental action must be seen not in terms of the human subject acting on or for the environment as object but in terms of a partnership or collaboration between the two. More recent engagements in ecology, philosophy, and religious studies include Donna J. Haraway, *When Species Meet* (Minneapolis: University of Minnesota Press, 2008), 11, 295, et passim; Catherine Keller, *Political Theology of the Earth: Our Planetary Emergency and the Struggle for a New Public* (New York: Columbia University Press, 2018), who also uses "anthropic exceptionalism"; and Dean, "'At Home on the Earth.'" For a provocative collection of essays by religionists exploring relations between the Bible, speciesism, and posthumanism, see also Jennifer L. Koosed, ed., *The Bible and Posthumanism*, Semeia Studies 74 (Atlanta: Society of Biblical Literature, 2014).

7. Sven Beckert, *Empire of Cotton: A Global History* (New York: Vintage, 2014), xv.

2: ONCE WE WERE LIKE GODS

1. In 1977, Christian musician LaVerne Tripp also released the long-play album called *Earth Born/Heaven Bound*, which included a song with the same title (QCA Records, 1977). For a video recording of Tripp and his family performing the song on television in 1980, see https://www.youtube.com/watch?v=4SlOpGoJe6E.

2. Francis Bacon, "An Advertisement Touching a Holy War," *The Works of Francis Bacon, Volume III: Works Political* (London: C. Baldwin, 1819), 485. In this fictional dialogue between four interlocutors, written in 1622, Bacon places these representations of the dominion verse as "charter of foundation" and "original donation of government" in the mouth of Zebedaeus. The extent to which Bacon himself agrees or disagrees with this character's arguments justifying colonial expansion in the Americas and Turkey as holy war is a matter of debate. See, e.g., Craig M. Rustici, "'The Great Sophism of All Sophisms': Colonialist Redefinition in Bacon's 'Holy War,'" *Renaissance and Reformation/Renaissance et Réforme* 16.4 (1992); and Jude Welburn, "Empire and Utopia: Images of the New World in Francis

Bacon's Works," *English Literary Renaissance* 48.2 (2018). Whether or not Bacon intended to identify fully with Zebedaeus's argument for holy war, his representation of the dominion verse is clearly consistent with Bacon's interpretations of this verse elsewhere.

3. Francis Bacon, *Novum Organum* II.52, in *The Works of Francis Bacon*, Volume IV.I, ed. and trans. J. Spedding, R. L. Ellis, and D. D. Heath (London: Longman and Company, 1848), 247–48. The Latin reads, "*Homo enim per lapsum et de statu innocentiae decidit, et de regno in creaturas. Utraque autem res etiam in hac vita nonnulla ex parte reparari potest; prior per religionem et fidem, posterior per artes et scientias,*" which I translate as follows: "For man, by the fall, was cut off from the state of innocence and from dominion in creation. Both things can in this life be partially repaired, the former by religion and faith, the latter by arts and sciences."

4. Francis Bacon, *Valerius Terminus*, in John M. Robertson, ed., *The Philosophical Works of Francis Bacon: Reprinted from the Texts and Translations with the Notes and Prefaces of Ellis and Spedding* (London: Routledge, 1905), 188–89.

5. Evelyn Fox Keller, *Reflections on Gender and Science*, 10th-ann. ed. (New Haven, CT: Yale University Press, 1995), 36.

6. Benjamin Farrington, "Temporis Partus Masculus: An Untranslated Writing of Francis Bacon," *Centaurus* 1 (1951): 197, 201.

7. I further unpack this theory of meme-like biblical circulation and "reception" in cultural history in *The Book of Revelation: A Biography* (Princeton, NJ: Princeton University Press, 2018), 4–10 and 222–23.

8. John William Fletcher, *American Patriotism: Farther Confronted with Reason, Scripture, and the Constitution* (London, 1776), 36.

9. John Locke, *Two Treatises on Civil Government* (London: George Routledge and Sons, 1884), II.V., 29–32.

10. Beckert, *Empire of Cotton*, xv–xvi.

11. Gary Snyder, *The Practice of the Wild: Essays* (New York: Farrar, Straus and Giroux, 1990), 12.

12. Samuel Martin, "The Instincts of Industry," *Twelve Lectures Delivered Before the Young Men's Christian Association, in Exeter Hall, from December 1850, to February 1851* (London: James Nisbet and Co., 1851), 466–69.

13. On early modern conceptions of animals as machines defined over against humans, esp. in Descartes, and the existential anxieties such conceptions belie, see esp. Jacques Derrida, *The Animal That Therefore I Am*, ed. Marie-Louise Mallet, trans. David Wills, Perspectives in Continental Philosophy (New York: Fordham University Press, 2008).

14. Walter Brueggemann, "Choosing Against Chosenness," in *Tenacious Solidarity: Biblical Provocations on Race, Religion, Climate, and the Economy*, ed. and intro. Davis Hankins (Minneapolis: Fortress, 2018), 124–25.

15. An excellent resource for exploring how the conquest narratives in the biblical book of Joshua have been leveraged in relation to colonialism, the military expropriation of Native lands, and the genocidal "othering" of Indigenous peoples is the sidebar series "Indigeneity Under Threat," in Carolyn J. Sharp, *Joshua* (Macon, GA: Smyth & Helwys, 2019).

16. See Keller, *Political Theology of the Earth*, which traces the "multi-temporary series of intersecting exceptionalisms" (73), from Anglo-Saxon exceptionalism to white supremacism and American exceptionalism, unfolding in an "absolute investment in the extractivism and exterminism that pump the global economy" (14).

17. Ludwig Feuerbach, *The Essence of Christianity*, trans. Marian Evans (New York: Calvin Blanchard, 1855), 355–56.

18. Stephen Toulmin, *Cosmopolis: The Hidden Agenda of Modernity* (Chicago: University of Chicago Press, 1990).

3: WE ARE THE GODS NOW

1. Unless otherwise indicated, all translations of biblical passages are my own.

2. Feuerbach, *The Essence of Christianity*, 6, 7.

3. Friedrich Nietzsche, *The Anti-Christ*, trans. R.J. Hollingdale (London: Penguin, 1968), section 48.

4. Stewart Brand, *The Whole Earth Catalog*, Fall 1968. Later issues substituted "we might as well get *used to* it" with "we might as well get *good at* it." The full statement of purpose in this first issue was as follows: "We *are* as gods and might as well get used to it. So far, remotely done power and glory—as via government, big business, formal education, church—has succeeded to the point where gross [defects] obscure actual gains. In response to this dilemma and to these gains, a realm of intimate, personal power is developing—power of the individual to conduct his own education, find his own inspiration, shape his own environment, and share his adventure with whoever is interested."

5. Edmund Leach, *A Runaway World*, Lecture 1: Men and Nature, The Reith Lectures, first aired November 12, 1967, BBC Radio 4. Published in book form as Edmund Leach, *A Runaway World? Reith Lectures 1967* (London: British Broadcasting Corporation, 1968).

6. Leach, *A Runaway World*, Lecture 1.

7. To be sure, this deep ambivalence in response to the prospect of closing the distance between humankind and divinity is not new. Indeed, as we know, the biblical God planted the seeds of this ambivalence by banishing Eve and Adam from Paradise for fear that they would otherwise "become like one of us" and, a little later, by razing the Tower of Babel and scattering its inhabitants, because "this is only the beginning of what they will do;

nothing that they propose to do will now be impossible for them" (Genesis 11:6; New Revised Standard Version).

8. For an outstanding and deeply thoughtful exploration of major figures in the transhumanist movement, see esp. Mark O'Connell, *To Be a Machine: Adventures Among Cyborgs, Utopians, Hackers, and the Futurists Solving the Modest Problem of Death* (New York: Anchor Books, 2017). My treatment here is very much indebted to this book and its insights, esp. chapter 4, "Once Out of Nature."

9. Max More, "A Letter to Mother Nature," first presented at the EXTRO 4: Biotechs Future conference in Berkeley, California, in August 1999, and available on More's website at http://strategicphilosophy.blogspot.com/2009/05/its-about-ten-years-since-i-wrote.html.

10. Jason Silva, "We Are the Gods Now," Festival of Dangerous Ideas, Sydney, Australia, September 2012, https://youtu.be/cF2VrefjIjk. Silva arrives at this position, surprisingly enough, from a discussion of Ernest Becker's *The Denial of Death*, which we will explore at length in the next chapter. After rejecting religion and romantic love as possible solutions, Silva embraces creative engineering through science and technology as the true means of denying and transcending death. Becker, as we will see, would disagree, and would argue, as I do, that all of these "immortality vehicles," including Silva's, are fundamentally religious.

11. Marshall McLuhan, *Understanding Media: The Extensions of Man* (Cambridge, MA: MIT Press, 1994); first published in 1964. Compare Silva, "What Is the Future of Us?" A-Fest Bali 2019, Mindvalley Talks, https://youtu.be/1-Rr-QXQt5I: "Our tools are extensions of our cognitive apparatus. They are appendages of our mind. They are our exoskeleton."

12. Ray Kurzweil, *The Singularity Is Near: When Humans Transcend Biology* (New York: Viking, 2005), 7.

13. Kurzweil, *The Singularity Is Near*, 9.

14. Kurzweil, *The Singularity Is Near*, 10.

15. Kurzweil, *The Singularity Is Near*, 9; emphasis added.

16. Kurzweil, *The Singularity Is Near*, 390.

17. O'Connell, *To Be a Machine*, 75–76. There are also parallels between Kurzweil's vision of the Singularity and process theology in the tradition of Teilhard de Chardin, especially his idea of the Omega Point, which refers to the ultimate level of complexity into which the universe will evolve.

18. Andy Clark, *Natural-Born Cyborgs: Minds, Technologies, and the Future of Human Intelligence* (New York: Oxford University Press, 2003), 198.

19. O'Connell, *To Be a Machine*, 63. See also John Gray, *To Be a Marionette: A Short Inquiry into Human Freedom* (New York: Farrar, Straus, and Giroux, 2015), 10: "Unknown to those who most ardently profess it, the boldest secular thinkers are possessed by a version of mystical religion."

At present, Gnosticism is the faith of people who believe themselves to be machines."

20. Jussi Parikka, *A Geology of Media*, Electronic Mediations 46 (Minneapolis: University of Minnesota Press, 2015); and Kate Crawford, *Atlas of AI: Power, Politics, and the Planetary Costs of Artificial Intelligence* (New Haven: Yale University Press, 2021).

21. Crawford, *Atlas of AI*, 11.

4: GODS WITH ANUSES

1. My translation. Unless otherwise indicated, biblical translations are my own.

2. Søren Kierkegaard, *The Concept of Anxiety: A Simple Psychologically Orienting Deliberation on the Dogmatic Issue of Hereditary Sin*, trans. and ed. Reidar Thomte with Albert B. Anderson, Kierkegaard's Writings, VIII (Princeton, NJ: Princeton University Press, 1980), 25–45.

3. Ernest Becker, *The Denial of Death* (New York: Free Press, 1997), 282–83.

4. Becker, *The Denial of Death*, 26.

5. Becker, *The Denial of Death*, 50. In the book, written in 1973, Becker's gender-exclusive language and masculine examples are deeply problematic, even if his insights about the denial of death are not. The Ernest Becker Foundation, which "does not endorse such regressive views and recognizes and supports gender equality as a fundamental human right," seeks to promote "dialogue about the problematic aspects of Becker's work in regard to feminist issues, and explore how Becker's insights inform our understanding of women's rights issues and unequal treatment." The foundation raises the possibility that "Becker's greatest contribution to the conversation about misogyny and the plight of women is how his insights have catalyzed work that integrates existential and feminist perspectives to examine the motivational underpinnings behind the patriarchy and women's rights issues today. . . . Becker's analyses help us explain why we don't like to talk about periods or see women breastfeed in public, why we objectify women, why women internalize the male gaze, why we love cleavage but don't like nipples, why men want to control women's reproductive rights, why a woman taking care of a dead body is a feminist act, and how patriarchal culture is facilitated" (https://ernestbecker.org/this-mortal-life/feminism).

6. Becker, *The Denial of Death*, 26.

7. Becker, *The Denial of Death*, 31, 33.

8. Becker, *The Denial of Death*, 51.

9. Becker, *The Denial of Death*, 172; explicating Otto Rank, *Art and Artist: Creative Urge and Personality Development* (New York: Agathon Press, 1968), 86.

10. Sam Keen, "Foreword" to Becker, *The Denial of Death*, xiii–xiv.

11. Becker, *The Denial of Death*, 159–60.

12. Becker, *The Denial of Death*, 5.

13. For a deeply insightful reflection on the clearing of the forest, which is there before and after our fleeting civilizations, see Robert Pogue Harrison, *Forests: The Shadow of Civilization* (Chicago: University of Chicago Press, 1993), chapter 1. This book, along with Gary Snyder's *The Practice of the Wild*, have accompanied me throughout most of my career as a teacher and writer.

14. Although Becker delivered the manuscript of *The Denial of Death* to his publisher in November 1972, a month before he was diagnosed with colon cancer, there is reason to believe that he was aware of being gravely ill months before while working in earnest on the book. See Jack Martin and Daniel Liechty, "Ernest Becker's Dark Turn (1971–1973): A Critical 'Deepening,'" *Journal of Humanistic Psychology* 59 (2019): esp. 140–43; and J. Martin, "Ernest Becker at Simon Fraser University (1969–1974)," *Journal of Humanistic Psychology* 54 (2014): 96–97.

15. Becker, *The Denial of Death*, 281–82. Becker saw models for this kind of openness among the religious, especially in "those extrasensitive types who have filled the roles of shaman, prophet, saint, poet, and artist." Infused with wonder and awe, fascination and fear, he writes, they are "alive to the panic inherent in creation."

5: PALLIATIVE HOPE

1. Atul Gawande, "Letting Go: What Should Medicine Do When It Can't Save Your Life?," *New Yorker*, August 2, 2010; also Atul Gawande, *Being Mortal: Illness, Medicine, and What Matters in the End* (New York: Henry Holt, 2014).

2. B. J. Miller, "What Really Matters at the End of Life," TED Talk, March 2015, https://www.ted.com/talks/bj_miller_what_really_matters_at_the_end_of_life? See also B. J. Miller and Shoshana Berger's very practical and very gracious *A Beginner's Guide to the End: Practical Advice for Living Life and Facing Death* (New York: Simon & Schuster, 2019).

3. On consumerism as "terror management," understood in the tradition of Becker, see, e.g., S. Solomon, J. L. Greenberg, and T. A. Pyszczynski, "Lethal Consumption: Death-Denying Materialism," in *Psychology and Consumer Culture: The Struggle for a Good Life in a Materialistic World*, ed. T. Kasser and A.D. Kanner (Washington, DC: American Psychological Association, 2004), 127–46.

4. Naomi Klein, *This Changes Everything: Capitalism vs. the Planet* (New York: Simon and Schuster, 2014), 3–4.

5. I draw inspiration for this approach from two directions, one that is new to me and one that has shaped my thinking throughout my

career. The former is Jonathan Lear's *Radical Hope: Ethics in the Face of Cultural Devastation* (Cambridge, MA: Harvard University Press, 2008), a philosophical-anthropological exploration of the possibility of hope after the end of a civilization based on the story of the Crow nation. Lear argues that such a community, living after the end of life as they have known it, needs a *poet*, that is, a "creative maker of meaningful space" (51) who can remake a new way of life from the ruins of what has been lost, providing "the imaginative tools with which to endure a conceptual onslaught" (78–79). The latter is the late feminist ecotheologian Sallie McFague, whose theoretical work (e.g., *Metaphorical Theology: Models of God in Theological Language* [Philadelphia: Fortress Press, 1982) argued that all theological language is metaphorical and, at its best, "tensive, discontinuous, and surprising" (14). This early work opened up onto a series of theological explorations of new metaphors for the divine that break down both patriarchal models of God and ecologically harmful dualisms between God and the world (e.g., *Models of God: Theology for an Ecological, Nuclear Age* [Philadelphia: Fortress Press, 1987]; *The Body of God: An Ecological Theology* [Minneapolis: Fortress Press, 1993]; and *A New Climate for Theology: God, the World, and Global Warming* [Minneapolis: Fortress Press, 2008]). Taking Lear and McFague together, I find a call for the poetic making of imaginative theological spaces, drawing on new metaphors and on the ruins of inherited dead ones.

6. I think of this way of conceiving the human in relation to the rest of the world as an ancient anticipation of object-oriented ontology (OOO) and speculative realism, which aim to decenter anthropocentrism, conceiving humans as objects among and in relation to other objects. For a clear and thorough introduction, see Graham Harman, *The Quadruple Object* (Winchester, UK: Zero Books, 2011). See also the vibrant materialism of Jane Bennett, *Vibrant Matter: A Political Ecology of Things* (Durham, NC: Duke University Press, 2010).

7. Bron Taylor, *Dark Green Religion: Nature, Spirituality, and the Planetary Future* (Berkeley: University of California Press, 2010), 13. Taylor himself does not find potential resources in Christianity, and Judaism because he believes that their worldviews are incompatible with, indeed antithetical to, dark green religion.

6: BACK TO THE BEGINNINGS

1. In Job 38, which is part of God's speech from the whirlwind, the first act of creation involves a conflict between God and Sea (Hebrew *Yam*, appearing here without a definite article, as a proper name), who is a personification of the formless, watery deep that was there before the world began. God holds Yam back, swaddling it in clouds like a cranky baby, and then sinks Earth's foundations into its waters like some huge primeval

offshore drilling station. In Psalm 74, the creator God's struggle to establish order against chaos is much more intense: God first slays Leviathan and the sea dragons, who are monstrous forces of primordial chaos, in order to create the cosmos as a safe, orderly ecology for humans (contrast Psalm 104, in which Leviathan is not a monstrous opponent of creation but a celebrated sea creature with whom God plays). And in Proverbs 8, the creator God is accompanied by a divine female cohort, Wisdom (Hebrew *hokmah*), who declares that she was with God from the beginning of creation. To be clear, these poetic renderings do not offer full narrative accounts of creation; rather, they refer to them as if they would have been familiar to their audiences.

2. Or better, "*as* the image of God," on which see below.

3. Ironically, Bacon and other early modern champions of empirical observation seem also to have overlooked the observable differences in these two creation stories, conflating them into a single founding myth of the modern master narrative of human (Western, Christian, white) exceptionalism: created in the image of God and commanded to fill, subdue, and dominate creation (first story), banished from Paradise (second story) but with the God-given potential (first story) to regain their original place there (second story).

4. A third potential supporting text, also echoing Genesis 1, is Genesis 9:1–3, in which God tells the handful of survivors after the flood to "be fruitful and multiply and fill the earth," saying that fear and dread of them would fill all other animals, who would now be available to them for food.

5. For much fuller, more detailed scholarly analyses and interpretations of this and other Hebrew biblical texts in relation to their sociohistorical and environmental contexts from an ecological perspective, see esp. William P. Brown, *The Seven Pillars of Creation: The Bible, Science, and the Ecology of Wonder* (Oxford: Oxford University Press, 2010); Ronald A. Simkins, *Creation and Ecology: The Political Economy of Ancient Israel and the Environmental Crisis* (Eugene, OR: Cascade Books, 2020); David G. Horrell, *The Bible and the Environment: Towards a Critical Ecological Biblical Theology* (New York: Routledge, 2014); Theodore Hiebert, *The Yahwist's Landscape: Nature and Religion in Ancient Israel* (New York: Oxford University Press, 1996); and Daniel Hillel, *The Natural History of the Bible: An Environmental Exploration of the Hebrew Scriptures* (New York: Columbia University Press, 2007). For a Christian ecotheological engagement of biblical literature in relation to our ecological crisis by a biblical scholar, see esp. Patricia K. Tull, *Inhabiting Eden: Christians, the Bible, and the Ecological Crisis* (Louisville: Westminster John Knox Press, 2013).

6. The Latin Vulgate, which would have been close to the Latin text Augustine knew, reads "*In principio creavit Deus caelum et terram. Terra autem erat inanis et vacua . . .*" ("First, God created heaven and earth. Earth

was void and vacuous . . ."). The Greek Septuagint, which was a primary source for Latin translations, reads similarly: "*En arche epoiesen ho Theos ton ouranon kai ten gen. He de ge en aoratos kai akataskeuastos* . . . ("In the beginning, God made the heaven and the earth. And the earth was unseeable and unformed . . .").

7. David M. Carr, *Genesis 1-11*, International Exegetical Commentary on the Old Testament; Kindle edition (Stuttgart: Kohlhammer Verlag, 2021), 92; and Hermann-Josef Stipp, "Dominium terrae. Die Herrschaft der Menschen über die Tiere in Gen 1,26.28," in *Alttestamentliche Studien. Arbeiten zu Priesterschrift, Deuteronomistischem Geschichtswerk und Prophetie* (Berlin: De Gruyter, 2013), 59–86.

8. In his critical reflections on his work as a translator of the Common English Bible (2011), Theodore Hiebert, "Retranslating Genesis 1–2 Reconnecting Biblical Thought and Contemporary Experience," *Bible Translator* 70 (2019): 267, argues that being made in the image of God and commanded to rule over other animals in this text does not mean that they were given some kind of "unique divine essence or substance that separates them from the earth and from the rest of its life. Rather, the image of God gives humans a unique role or function, the role of being a divine representative on earth. . . . Humans' primary biblical vocation is to be responsible for the world as God would be."

9. Carr, *Genesis 1–11*, 59, following scholars who argue that "both literary context and Near Eastern parallels suggest that the preposition [*bet*] here is not a *bet normae* (e.g., 'in the image of God') but a *bet essentiae* (e.g., 'as the image of God') that is focused on the human role *as* divine representative on earth. Nevertheless, one should be careful here not to develop a false either/or, where a primary focus on human status 'as' images of God excludes the idea that this status is embodied by some human similarity to a God that is conceived along anthropomorphic lines."

7: HUMUS BEING

1. On the subsistence-based agricultural context of this story and its implications for translation and interpretation, see esp. Hiebert, *The Yahwist's Landscape*. Hiebert, "Retranslating Genesis 1–2," also argues convincingly for reading *'afar* in this context not as "dust" (the common translation) but as "topsoil."

2. Phyllis Trible, in her pioneering book *God and the Rhetoric of Sexuality* (Philadelphia: Fortress Press, 1978), 75–80. The earliest use of the phrase "humus being" that I can find is in an inaugural column entitled "Humus" in the March 2, 1977, issue of *Sagamore*, the student paper of Indiana University–Purdue University Indianapolis (archived at https://archives.iupui.edu/bitstream/handle/2450/10127/Sag19770302.pdf). The unidentified author elaborates many English words related to "humus,"

including, of course, "human," but does not mention the parallel relation of *'adam* and *'adamah* in Hebrew. The author writes, "Why, your very connotative description is a derivative from that oft-time 'dirtified' word humus. That's right, the word is really humus being. Now, don't you feel dirty?"

3. The verb form appears only three times, all in the passive Niphal form (Exodus 23:12; 31:17; and 2 Samuel 16:14). While often translated as "refreshed," a more literal translation might be "took a breather" or even "rebreathed."

4. For a helpful discussion of this term in relation to other terms in Hebrew biblical anthropology (e.g., *basar*/"flesh," *ruah*/"breath," *lev*/"heart"), see esp. Hans Schwartz, *The Human Being: A Theological Anthropology* (Grand Rapids, MI: Wm. B. Eerdmans Publishing, 2013), 5–10, which is closely engaged with the influential work by Hans Walter Wolff, *Anthropology of the Old Testament*, trans. Margaret Kohl (Philadelphia: Fortress Press, 1974). Against Wolff, Schwartz proposes that *nefeš* can be synonymous with the self, "I," as in Psalm 16:10, "do not abandon my *nefeš* [often translated "me"] to Sheol" (interestingly, Schwartz makes the same argument for *basar*, "flesh," as a term for self). For a recent discussion of the range of meanings of this word in relation to a network of related terms and phrases as they pertain to animals, see Richard Whitekettle, "A Study in Scarlet: The Physiology and Treatment of Blood, Breath, and Fish in Ancient Israel," *Journal of Biblical Literature* 135 (2016): 685–704, DOI: 10.15699/jbl.1354.2016.3091.

5. Biblical descriptions of dying as exhaling one's last breath include 1 Kings 17:21–22; Job 11:20, 31:39; and Genesis 35:18.

6. Whereas the ground that drinks wellspring water in Genesis 2 is *'adamah*, the term here and in most other texts, especially as they relate to the promised land, is *'ereṣ*.

7. See esp. Walter Brueggemann, *The Land*, rev. ed., Overtures to Biblical Theology (Philadelphia: Fortress Press, 2002), 59. See also his *Sabbath as Resistance: Saying No to the Culture of Now* (Louisville: Westminster John Knox, 2014).

8. Wendell Berry, "The Gift of Good Land," *The Gift of Good Land: Further Essays Cultural and Agricultural* (Berkeley, CA: Counterpoint, 2009), 271.

9. Note that "form" in this psalm is *yeṣer*, related to the verb *yaṣar*, which was used to describe God forming the human from the earth in Genesis 2:8. See also Isaiah 40:24; 51:12; and Psalm 102:3–4 and 11, in which the psalmist compares their days to passing smoke and declares their heart to be "withered like grass." Still other biblical texts conceive of humans not as short-lived vegetation but as short-lived animals: swarms of grasshoppers or locusts who disappear in the morning heat (Isaiah 40:22–24; Nahum 3:15–17).

10. This humbling reality is sometimes expressed with force, as in Isaiah's pronouncement against the empire of Babylon, who had presumed to ascend to heaven and become a god but who now lies in the ground upon a bed of maggots with worms for covers (Isaiah 14:11–15). Cf. Job 21:26, where the high and the lowly "lie down in dust together, and maggots cover them," and Job 25:5–6, where Bildad calls humans themselves maggots and worms. See also Ecclesiasticus 10:9–11 (NRSV): "How can dust and ashes be proud? / Even in life the human body decays. / A long illness baffles the physician; / the king of today will die tomorrow. / For when one is dead / he inherits maggots and vermin and worms."

8: NO HOPE WITHOUT GRIEF

1. Marissa Evans, "The Relentlessness of Black Grief," *Atlantic*, September 27, 2021, https://www.theatlantic.com/ideas/archive/2020/09/relentlessness-black-grief/616511.

2. Resmaa Menakem, *My Grandmother's Hands: Racialized Trauma and the Pathway to Mending Our Hearts and Bodies* (Las Vegas: Central Recovery Press, 2017), 4, 10.

3. Willie Jennings, "My Anger, God's Righteous Indignation," *For the Life of the World*, podcast episode 13, June 2, 2020, Yale Center for Faith and Culture, https://for-the-life-of-the-world-yale-center-for-faith-culture.simplecast.com/episodes/my-anger-gods-righteous-indignation-willie-jennings-response-to-the-death-of-george-floyd-FXkkWh9b/transcript. Italics added.

4. Cathleen Kaveny, *Prophecy Without Contempt: Religious Discourse in the Public Square* (Cambridge, MA: Harvard University Press, 2016), argues that effective rhetorical deployment of the prophetic jeremiad in political and legal discourse foregrounds grief and sympathy for the one under indictment. She emphasizes four key elements of prophetic rhetoric: judgment is against one's own nation (Israel/Judah), the prophet stands with those under indictment, the prophet expresses sorrow for those being judged, and the prophet situates judgment on the horizon of hope.

5. For a thorough and insightful examination of this biblical theme, see esp. Katherine M. Hayes, *"The Earth Mourns": Prophetic Metaphor and Oral Aesthetic*, Academia Biblica, Volume 8 (Leiden: Brill, 2002). Hayes focuses specifically on the nine prophetic passages that refer to *'ereṣ* ("earth" or "land") alongside the verb *'aval*, usually translated as "mourn" (but also meaning "dry up"). These passages are Amos 1:2; Joel 1:5–20; Isaiah 24:1–20; Isaiah 33:7–9; Jeremiah 12:1–4; Jeremiah 12:7–13; Jeremiah 4:23–28; Jeremiah 23:9–12; and Hosea 4:1–3. Hayes argues convincingly for the coherence of this metaphor and expression as a persistent poetic image and theological idea in Israelite and Judean history. While my focus here is broader than this formal category, I find her analyses astute and compelling.

6. See also Isaiah 24:1–20, a so-called proto-apocalyptic poem that envisions the earth or land in a process of uncreation, being emptied of its inhabitants and returning to primordial chaos. There the earth is described as lamenting, languishing, faltering, and stumbling, burdened as it is from the weight of human injustices. Other prophetic texts in which social injustice correlates with ecological and cosmological breakdown include the following: Hosea 4:3, which describes the people stealing, lying, murdering, and so on, and then very abruptly conjures a land mourning in the midst of mass extinction, including not only its human inhabitants but all animal life: "Over this the land mourns ['aval] / and all who dwell in it languish [yabeš]. Along with the animals of the field and the birds of the air / and the fish of the sea, they die"; Jeremiah 23:9–12, in which sin and disobedience lead to a cursed state for which "the land mourns ['aval], and the pastures of the wilderness are dried up [yabeš]"; Amos 8:4–8, which paints a vivid picture of his people's injustices (they "trample the needy" and "bring an end to the poor in the land" by inflating prices and using false balances; they "buy the poor for silver and the needy for a pair of sandals," selling them floor sweepings to eat) and then imagines the land racked in anguish not only *for* its doomed inhabitants but *along with* them; and Micah 7:13, in which "the earth will be desolate [šamam]," connoting both physical desolation and the psychic desolation of mourning, "because of its inhabitants, / for the fruit of their doings" (NRSV).

7. But cf. Isaiah 10:23: "For the lord, LORD of hosts, has decided to make a complete ending [kalah] in all the earth." Still other prophetic texts that can be read to demonstrate this capacity to imagine a world without humans include Isaiah 6:11–12, 13:9; Jeremiah 7:33, 24:10, 25:12; Ezekiel 33:28; Zechariah 7:14; and Zephaniah 1.

9: SUBSISTENTIALISM

1. The classic and still prescient critique of this construction is Simone de Beauvoir's *The Second Sex*, trans. H. M. Parshley, first published in 1949 (New York: Vintage, 1989). Luce Irigaray, *Speculum of the Other Woman*, trans. G.G. Gill (Ithaca, NY: Cornell University Press, 1985), exposes the male/masculine subject's vulnerability and fragility, dependent as it is on his projection of the other woman as fixed object, over against which his own subjectivity is defined and secured.

2. Irigaray, *Speculum of the Other Woman*, 135.

3. I first encountered this spelling in John W. Harvey's translation of Rudolf Otto's *Idea of the Holy* (London: Oxford University Press, 1923), 40, where he describes "the monstrous" (*das Ungeheuere*) as "a fairly exact expression for the numinous in its aspects of mystery, awefulness, majesty, augustness, and 'energy'; nay, even the fascination is dimly felt in it."

4. Snyder, *The Practice of the Wild*, 154.

5. Snyder, *The Practice of the Wild*, 184–85.
6. Snyder, *The Practice of the Wild*, 184.
7. Jean-Paul Sartre, *Existentialism and Humanism*, trans. Philip Mairet (London: Methuen, 1948), 28.
8. Sartre, *Existentialism and Humanism*, 184.
9. Snyder, *The Practice of the Wild*, 93. See also the insightful chapters on these cultures as well as the Mistassini Cree and the Koyukon people in David Kinsley, *Ecology and Religion: Ecological Spirituality in Cross-Cultural Perspective* (Englewood Cliffs, NJ: Prentice Hall, 1995), 3–41.

EPILOGUE
1. "Greta Thunberg's Speech at the U.N. Climate Action Summit," September 23, 2019, available at https://www.npr.org/2019/09/23/763452863/transcript-greta-thunbergs-speech-at-the-u-n-climate-action-summit.
2. Isra Hirsi, "The Climate Movement Needs More People Like Me," *Grist*, March 25, 2019, https://grist.org/article/the-climate-movement-needs-more-people-like-me.
3. Xiye Bastida, "Message from Xiye Bastida," Flourishing Diversity Summit 2019, available at https://www.youtube.com/watch?v=2UBolyJHELk.

INDEX

aboriginal, biblical, 121–23
Abraham, 35, 37
Adam, 88
Adam and Eve, 26, 41, 42, 138n7
'adam, 95, 145n2
'adamah, 95, 145n2, 145n6
'afar, 89, 144n1
"After the Gold Rush" (Young), 70
agency, 48, 89, 93, 99
agriculture, 32, 84
Alaskan wood bison, 70
Amos, denial and, 105–6
anality, meaning of, 57–58
Anchorage Daily News, 115
anger, 126, 127; divine, 103; hope
    and, 103; righteous, 104
animality, 61, 118
animals, 26, 82, 85; humans and,
    117, 121; killing/eating, 83; as
    machines, 137n13; nonhuman,
    31, 82; survival of, 121; thriving
    of, 82
Anthropocene, 20, 43, 65; faith in,
    2–4; finding way in, 22–23; gods
    of, 53–54; religion of, 122, 123
Anthropocene Working Group, 2
anti-Semitism, 35
anxiety, 9, 67, 102
apocalypse, 102
apocalypticism, 14, 133n1
Arbery, Ahmaud, 101

artificial intelligence, 45, 53, 59
arts, practical/mechanical, 29
asteroid showers, 17, 18
Athabascan people, 70
atheism, 42
atomic bombs, 2
Augustine of Hippo, 80, 143n6
'avad, 89

Babylon, 35, 146n10
Bacon, Francis, 53; charter of foun-
    dation and, 19, 29; creation
    stories and, 143n3; dominion
    and, 30, 136n2; holy war and,
    137n2
basar, 145n4
Bastida, Xiye, 128, 129
Beal, Clay: coyote encounter and,
    112–13; memories of, 111–12
Beal, Clover, 13, 14
Beal, Gerri, 111–12
Beal, Jenny, 111, 112–13
Beal, Seth, 14
Beal, Sophie, 13–14, 22, 23, 125–26
bear, encounter with, 113–16
Becker, Ernest, 1, 58, 63, 72, 118,
    139n10, 141n14; anality and,
    57–58; Christianity and, 60;
    on creation/violence, 56;
    cultural systems and, 60–61;
    denial of death and, 4, 61;

gender-exclusive language of,
140n5; gods with anuses and,
58; misogyny and, 140n5; mortality and, 92; openness and,
141n15; on terror, 119; violence/
war and, 60
Beckert, Sven, 20, 32
bere'šit, 81
Berry, Wendell, 94
bet essentiae/bet normae, 144n9
Bible, 20, 22, 25; contradictions in,
77–78; defending, 77; as library
of questions, 6
biblical texts/stories, 30, 55, 75, 91;
engaging, 77–78
biblical tradition, 4, 5, 72, 104, 107
binaries, androcentric/anthropo-
centric, 117
biology, 2; transcending, 51, 68
biosphere, 119, 121
biotechnology, 47, 49
Black people: reparations for, 70;
violence against, 100, 101, 102
Blade Runner, 45
blessings, 10, 22, 25; divine, 29;
racial/economic inequalities of,
102; social/material, 37; special,
35, 63, 100, 103, 106
Blue Planet Prize, 18
Brand, Stuart, 43–44, 45
Brueggemann, Walter: biblical
prophets and, 10; on chosenness, 36; military consumerism
and, 135n10; Sabbath and, 94
Butler, Octavia, 17–18

Cain and Abel, 89
Canaan, 35, 36, 37
capitalism, 2, 19, 53, 61, 62; free
markets and, 33, 36; global, 4,
59, 75; industrial, 32; mercantile, 20; missionary networks
and, 33; war, 20, 32, 33

carbon dioxide emissions, 15, 16,
135n1
Carr, David M., 83, 84
Cave, Nick, 8, 9, 10
Chappelle, Dave, 104
charter of foundation, 29–35, 41, 55
Chauvin, Derek, 101, 104
"Choosing Against Chosenness"
(Brueggemann), 36
chosenness, 100, 103; American,
36; Christian, 35, 36; claims
to, 35–36; dominion and, 38;
entitlement and, 37; exclusion
and, 37; extraction and, 37–38;
Israelite, 36; racism and, 36;
violence and, 35–38
Christianity, 20, 26, 61, 73, 75, 123,
142n7; denial of death and, 1;
ecological crisis and, 134n6; as
immortality vehicle, 60; inherited traditions and, 5; missionary networks of, 33; scriptural
traditions of, 122; secret truth
of, 42; undoing, 42
civil rights, 101
civilization: collapse of, 18, 142n5;
ruined, 62; science/money/
goods and, 61; threats to, 33
Clark, Andy, 51
classism, environmental, 128
climate activists, 126–29
climate change, 3, 15–16, 71, 128
climate crisis, 9, 17, 21, 75, 126, 127
climate justice, 126, 128
colonialism, 2, 29, 38, 136n2,
138n15
communism, 60, 61
consciousness: creation and, 56;
expanding, 56; false, 52; godlike, 57
consumerism, 61; military, 135n10;
as terror management, 141n3;
transhumanism and, 69